A Chaos of Cats

A Chaos of Cats

A memoir of a man and his cats

William Lee

Illustrations by Kathy Wyatt

HODDER &
STOUGHTON

British Library Cataloguing in Publication Data
A record for this book is available from the British Library

ISBN-10: 0 340 908378
ISBN-13: 978 0340 90837 2

Printed and bound in Great Britain by Clays Ltd, St Ives plc

The paper used in this book is a natural recyclable product
made from wood grown in sustainable forests. The hard
coverboard is recycled.

Hodder & Stoughton
A Division of Hodder Headline Ltd
338 Euston Road
London NW1 3BH
www.madaboutbooks.com

Contents

1
The observation of cats

There is considerable wisdom to be gleaned from the observation of cats.

They can be observed in peace and quiet in the comfort of one's own home, in the manner of watching television or enjoying a video or just flopping around on the sofa eating ice-cream and staring vacantly into space. This is something so many of us so often do, practically without even thinking about it, and many of us do extremely well.

Or they can be observed in the familiar and relaxing atmosphere of one's garden, with the added inducement of something not necessarily non-alcoholic at one's side and the consoling thought that one is not simply lounging around the garden doing nothing when one should be doing the washing and ironing, but learning from the great book of Nature.

In other words, cats are not only interesting creatures in their own right, an opinion with which they would be the very first to agree, but they are also great excuses for not doing things that, strictly speaking, we really should be doing – something for which we should be extremely thankful. Not all animals have this particular skill: indeed, if the truth were told, most do not, and if I am offending any of them I apologise immediately and without reserve, especially to the big, toothy ones.

Cats are wonderful and mysterious creatures them-selves in their own small, furry way. When one sees them staring into space with a meditative, faraway look in their eyes, it is difficult to decide whether they are contemplating the great imponderables of the universe or have caught an interesting smell of cooking coming over from next door, and are asking themselves whether or not to take the risk of creeping through the neighbours' open pantry window to sample whatever it is that is going. They know that the neighbours can be quite unpredictable and irrational, especially when there is a bit of bad feeling going on between them and their own household over some silly misunderstanding or other, quite possibly (indeed, highly probably) caused by the felines themselves.

And this, indeed, is the essence of cat. Cats may be solving some of the great philosophical questions of the ages, to their own satisfaction and, potentially, also to ours, or they may be simply thinking about their stomachs and the sort of things they would ideally like to be putting into them. Or, even more prosaically, they may simply just be thinking about a flea. We can never really be quite sure, and this doubt is yet another of the great tantalising problems of existence of the very sort that cats seem so good at solving.

2
A little history (1)
How we ended up with cats

It is quite possibly the better part of a hundred thousand years, give or take a decade, since people started asking themselves the question: how is it we ended up with cats and dogs as our domestic companions in this vale of tears? How is it we didn't set our hearts on cuddly little weasels or skunks or wombats or duck-billed platypus? (platypuses? platypusses? platypi? platypussies?) Well, in the case of the duck-billed platypus the answer is clear – they had been cut off, through no fault of their own, by the Drift of Continents, and would not have made very promising house-pets, being all worked up about exactly what branch of the animal kingdom they belonged to. There is also the aggravating factor that, as I have just demonstrated, no one can really be sure as to their plural form, which is a very embarrassing thing for any animal and is probably why they prefer to be found alone. As we all know, an animal with an identity crisis reaching back into the murky mists of time is most certainly not to be recommended, especially when there are small children around.

I have pondered this question about how we ended up with cats and dogs a great deal, and I have also discussed it with the experts up the pub, and, after discarding some of the more outrageous hypotheses, we did finally come to what seems to be a fairly viable conclusion. We believe that people started living with cats before they took up with dogs. We know that all the dogs will start barking and yelling and saying what a cruel and hurtful thing this is to say, but we believe they started with cats because of all the mice. It is more than probable that our ancestors' caves were absolutely heaving with rats and mice because of all the bones and things they used to throw in the corners and kick under the bearskins and rude trestles and other primitive items of furniture.

The cavemen probably tried all sorts of solutions to get rid of these pests before turning to the animal kingdom for help, and one can only imagine the sort of fun and games that went on in those caves during the long millennia of trial and error. Probably different kinds of monkeys would have been recruited, but it would only have taken a few centuries for our slow-thinking ancestors to realise that monkeys, as mousers, are practically hopeless. Other creatures, such as rabbits and squirrels perhaps, may also have been tried out, with equally dismal results. And it is quite possible that if our ancestors had actually got round to inventing the broom, our long and intimate relationship with cats might never even have got started at all.

What probably happened is that one fine day one of these cavemen came in from his hunting and/or gathering or, perhaps more likely, fishing, with a nice big ginger cat in a hairy bag, and loosed it in the cave just to see what would happen. That cat would have allowed a split second for his eyes to adjust to the penumbra of the cave and his nostrils to accommodate themselves to the rather rich odour that characterised Stone Age dwellings. Then he would have spotted a shadow flitter across the wall. 'Ahah,' he would have thought, 'Ah hah.' And his eyes would have started bulging and his nose would have started twitching and his whiskers would have started bristling and his mouth would have started drooling and chirruping uncontrollably and he would have been thinking, 'Wow, what a place! Nice of that two-legged stinking individual there to invite me back for dinner. Didn't like being stuck in that smelly hairy bag, though. Hasn't he got a cat-carrier? Wow! What on earth was that coming out of that hole?'

And the rest, as the saying goes, is history.

3

How one obtains cats

It is theoretically possible for cats to just materialise out of nothing and wander, purring loudly, tail pointing heavenwards as if to insinuate that this is their place of origin, into one's life. My own very first cat, when I still lived with Mum and Dad, was a ginger-and-white incarnation of sheer cheek and charisma, perfect shirt-front and spats and a devil-may-care buccaneer self-assurance. He just strolled in from the garden one bright morning, cool as you please. He started chatting away to us in a rich, high-pitched staccato miaow, as if he had known us all his life, about heaven only knows what. His blarney entirely captivated us, as it was clearly intended to do, and we watched open-mouthed as he ambled across the sitting-room carpet, popped himself into our most comfortable armchair with the air of one saying, 'Just give me a call when lunch is served, would you, old boy?' and never went away again.

I have often felt that that rare thing, the cat who just comes along out of no-where and moves in and adopts you (rather than you adopting it from a friend or relative or animal shelter or pushy acquaintance or whatever) is, in its way, a most particular blessing. He or she has chosen you, you out of the whole wide world, and, having done so, will be loyal and faithful to you to the end. Cats Who Just Arrive Like That seldom, if ever, disappear again, but stick with you through thick and thin. They have chosen and will abide by their choice, while cats you yourself have adopted can – and it does happen – simply disappear, just move off somewhere else, just gather their things and move on, headed for

Reno or Salinas or Paris, France or the High Pamirs or indeed (why not?) Kathmandu, and it's 'Bye then, see you around,' and a kiss and a tear and a quick purr and a quick rub of their muzzle against your leg and that's that and they never turn up again. This is a curious and inexplicable thing, and it can be heartbreaking, but that's just the way some cats are. Well, we do that sort of thing, too, when you think about it, so we can hardly hold it against the cats.

It was probably precisely one of those globetrotting cats that turned up in my porch one rainy afternoon many years ago now. He was the classic old hellraiser of a cat, the sort that we pretend not to know when they miaow at us in the street, tatty and disreputable and flea-ridden and just a bit too cheeky and familiar. He looked all mud and blood and beer, dosshouses and bounced cheques, and there were so many odds and ends of fur and bits of ears and tail and things missing from him you'd swear he'd seen more action than the Life Guards. He was clearly very old, and had only half his teeth left and a couple of claws were gone, too. He was also completely deaf and very nearly blind: when you gazed into those big, bright old eyes of his all you saw was a kind of squinting opacity that was quite disarming. I cannot really say how old he was when he decided to adopt us to see him through the final stage of his clearly memorable and distinguished existence, but I'm prepared to take my oath he was a good twenty if he was a day, and that's good going, very good going, for a cat. Anyway, he just turned up, a grubby old ruin. I thought of some of my own cats who had chosen the road, and decided, 'Well, in you come.' And in he came, purring feebly, but purring.

My other cats, to their credit, simply sniffed around him a bit, idly curious, a couple of them just a touch on the snooty side, then made up their minds to leave him to his own devices – he was clearly too old for there to be any fun in him – showing no diffidence or hostility whatsoever towards him. They probably knew as well as I did that the poor old boy had instinctively decided our home was a safe haven for the final scene of his last act, for the last peaceful sunsets of his ninth life, and hospitably decided to welcome him among them, maybe not with drums and trumpets and fanfares but with good, classy, feline *laissez-faire*.

I myself was rather moved. I felt peculiarly flattered and highly complimented by what I still firmly believe to be a sublime example of feline trust and faith in human nature, a nature that, to tell the truth, has not over the centuries given all that much proof of actually meriting such faith, if you see what I mean. I mean, humans have often been not very nice where cats are concerned. Even in these more enlightened times our record is not quite impeccable, and I'm not just talking about abroad.

Anyway, he stayed with us for a matter of a few weeks, and we fed him and kept him nice and warm and gave him a comfy basket to sleep in and combed out his knotty old fur a bit and got rid of his fleas and brought him occasional savoury little treats – and God!, he had an appetite! And all he had to do was lie around sleeping and eating and purring and getting patted from time to time, happy as a sand boy, enjoying the warmth and coming out with a little contented cough every so often, like a miniature tattered old lion, just to remind us he was still with us.

When the time came, I remember that he licked my hand and gazed calmly into my eyes with his own poor, squinting, cloudy orbs, then ambled casually across the room from his basket and crawled under the dresser. I knew what he was doing. I let him do it. No fuss, no drama, no bother. He had adopted us for this, after all: to have a nice, safe place to wind up his long and active and busy life, and to have a warm and peaceful place to creep into when he felt it was time to go.

By the next day, of course, it was all over, just as I had known it would be when I saw him slip under that dresser. He had plenty of class, too, that old mog. But I wept like a child when I buried him, although it was a happy kind of weeping because I knew that, if cats don't get to heaven, he'd had a little bit of heaven anyway, with us, while getting ready for the night. And I wept because he had licked my hand to say thanks, before he went away, and I still believe that there can be fewer sweeter things than that.

4

How one becomes
a cat-lover (1)

Cat-lovers are not born, they are made. I remember that as a child I was, generally speaking, pretty indifferent to cats. But I have to admit, to my enduring shame, that when I got hold of one I was not above giving it a hard time. I used to see other, bigger boys throw stones at them, and worse, and I took it as quite natural that I should do the same. I remember – though I did not myself participate and I was too small to do anything about it – once seeing a group of very tough boys taking a cat up to the top of a four-storey building and throwing it out of the window to see if it had nine lives. Naturally, it didn't.

However, as I say, I am by no means blameless myself, and there are things I feel I have to confess to here, maybe in part as a sort of catharsis which, I hope, should purge me of the weight of past sins. Once I closed a nice little grey cat in a dustbin, and enjoyed myself giving hefty kicks to the bin and listening to the terrified yowls and screeches and frantic clawings and scratchings coming from inside. The bin was also full of stinking rubbish, which amused me even more. I was a mean little bastard. I know it now, and I know that, not very deep down, I knew it even then. But I do feel that there was little that was genuinely malicious or sadistic in what I was doing. It was much more just the foolish and misguided ignorance of a child who had been subject to bad examples, rather than anything radically malevolent in my nature.

I once sprayed pepper at the cat of my nice old neighbour, Mrs Dewar, then fell about laughing my head off at its antics. The poor thing leapt at least six feet into the air, spinning like a top, an absolute blur of speed, tried to scrabble up a wall, eyes popping, every hair of its fur standing on end, claws spread wide as fans, then collapsed like a wet rag, its eyes gushing, practically sneezing its heart out. The claw-marks remained on the wall for many years, a constant and implacable reminder of my guilt.

At the time, however, I felt it was a scream. Howling with laughter, absolutely yelling with mirth, I got ready to give it another good dusting, but I was gripping the little cardboard cylinder so tightly in my paroxysms that the lid shot right off, and instead of dusting the cat I dusted myself, getting a hefty dose in my eyes and in my mouth and right the way up my nose.

Suddenly I found myself identifying very profoundly with Mrs Dewar's cat. We made a lovely couple. There we were, sneezing and rolling and hopping up and down and hollering and yowling, a pair of perfectly synchronised dancing dervishes the two of us, red-eyed and with swollen noses and burning throats and rivers of mucus cascading out of us. I do believe I practically fainted with the pain, so I imagine Mrs Dewar's poor old cat did too. But one thing is sure and certain: I never harmed a cat again. I am happy to be able to report that I subsequently established a very amicable relationship with Mrs Dewar's cat (its name was Hopper) and we became very good friends and neighbours in the years to come. I must say, however, that Hopper would scrutinise me with a pretty hairy eyeball whenever he saw me holding anything that looked even remotely like a small orange cardboard cylinder. And whenever I saw that scared, wary look in his eyes and the unmistakable pose of a cat on its marks and ready to hit the horizon – ready, as it were, to hop it – I felt myself blush and cringe with repentance.

Old Hopper has been in his grave, under a cherry-blossom in Mrs Dewar's garden, a good many years now, but he lived a very long time. And I have sometimes speculated, perhaps in an attempt to allay the residues of guilt, whether that pepper experience did not have some sort of rejuvenating effect on the poor old fellow. Well, I mean, it's just possible, isn't it? One never knows, and thinking doesn't hurt.

5

How one becomes
a cat-lover (2)

Now, if there is one thing that can turn a teenager into
the most devoted cat-lover it is *giving one to a girl*.

Once upon a time, there used to be a girl who lived
down the road from me. She found out that my
parents had this cat who had given birth to kittens,
just at the time when her own family's cat had found
itself, with fatal consequences, under the wheels of the
milk float.

Even now, by the way, I still pause in disbelief and
doubt as I write this. All I can say is that that cat must
have been a real retard of a cat. But a cat actually
getting run over by a milk float . . . ?

Future generations will have absolutely no idea what a milk float really is, or was. But I can assure those future generations that the chances of a cat getting run over by a milk float are more or less the same as its getting itself hit smack in the middle of the face by a comet.

Anyway, this cat actually did manage to get itself run over by the milk float (thinking about it now, I wonder if it wasn't perhaps a particularly macabre and morbid form of feline suicide) just, as it happened, at the time when my own family had heaps and heaps of delightful kittens to give away to a deserving pet-loving family with garden.

Now the reader may, flatteringly, credit me with undue modesty when I say that the girl down the road did not like me one little bit. I hasten to assure the reader that undue modesty has absolutely nothing to do with it. The girl down the road could not stand me and used to make a face, or faces, when she saw me, as if I was something nameless and anomalous that she had found in a prawn-and-salad sandwich. When I approached her with an ingratiating smile she would run away as if I was a pack of hungry rogue Dobermans.

Painfully, I must now face up to the facts and acknowledge that there were various, very understandable, reasons for this extremist position. One of those reasons was spots, with which I was abundantly, indeed extravagantly, furnished. Spots, as every girl *down* the road knows, are a perfectly reasonable motive for not being able to stand the boy *up* the road. Another reason was dress-sense, something I did not have. And yet another reason, possibly the gravest, was bodily uncleanliness, in the sense that I was a bit of a slob and a stinker.

I have been known to say that her nose was irresistible, and it was. As was all the rest of her, from the white-and-pink tips and bows of her trainers to the pink ribbons in her golden hair. No, I will go further. The girl down the road was an absolute, mind-blowing, dream-wrecking cataclysmic *cracker*. And I do not mean your common-or-garden nice-bit-of-stuff-but-seen-it-all-before, or anything like that. As well as the face and the hair and the unbelievable smile (never directed at me, but I did get to see it from time to time, and it beat the sun hollow, especially when she'd just washed her hair), this is the girl who actually invented curves and legs.

Anyway, the simple fact of the matter is that her family found itself catless just at a time when my own family found itself, as it were, catful. We had a nice little she-cat in those days who had absolutely no morals and knew nothing about contraception or the morning-after pill (and wouldn't have bothered her head about it even if she had), and the result was that there were often kittens.

The girl down the road's mum, who got on quite well with my mum, heard that we had all these kittens on our hands. She suggested that she might be willing to relieve us of something of the burden, to the tune of one kitten. We, of course, had no objections – we had so many kittens around that the presence or absence of one or two of them would have made very little difference to the general scenario. The girl was a bit snooty about it at first. She simply couldn't stomach the idea of taking anything whatsoever from a family to which I and all my defects belonged. Not very nice of her, nor was it very kind, but pretty girls can get away with murder, and she was wearing pink leg-warmers and white pleated mini-skirts in those days.

One day, she came round to our place with her mum while I was out, to check out the kits. Those kittens were little beauties, and her heart went out to one of them in particular, went out in a big way, and that was that. In the warmth of her spontaneous surrender to that little fellow, all her hostility towards me became very much of secondary importance. That is an example, of course, of what cats, even tiny little cats, can do when they put their minds to it.

The great thing was that the kittens weren't ready. They were still quite tiny and totally dependent on their mother, and it would be a good six weeks at least, declared my own mother, before she would allow them to leave her. I've thought a good bit about this over the years, and with the wisdom of hindsight I've come to the conclusion that my mother was not thinking only about the kittens, but also about her unhappy spotty son and his hopeless, and all-too-obvious, crush on the girl down the road.

Well, whether it was by chance or design, the thing worked a treat. The girl down the road was so utterly infatuated by the kitten she had chosen that she couldn't resist coming round to my house every afternoon to see how it was coming along. The consequences of this were, of course, inevitable. I learnt, belatedly it is true, to wash. I learnt that there were special soaps for spots that actually worked – it wasn't just advertiser's blurb. I learnt to combine the clothes I wore with a certain sense of colour and compatibility that turned me into quite something else, and I learnt that things like combs and shoe-polish and smart trainers existed, and that their use brought about highly positive effects and results.

I also learnt important things about communication. I learnt that it was quite possible to talk to the girl who drove you simply mad in something more than goggle-eyed tongue-tied monosyllables. The great thing here, of course, was that we had something in common. We had the kitten to talk about, and the progress it was making, and how friendly it was getting, and how funny it was when it was scared of something, the sort of tricks it got up to – all that sort of thing. And once we had broken the ice by talking about such fundamental matters as these, the rest was downhill all the way. I found, to my stunned disbelief at first, that she was, in fact, really as shy and insecure as I was. But soon we had no difficulty in just casually and almost unconsciously drifting from one subject to another, as if we had known each other all our lives. I found that I could actually look into her eyes and hold the look for several seconds at a time without starting to twitch and drool and yodel. And then I could just open my mouth and grin (teeth well brushed and sparkling) and come out with whatever nonsense came into my head and it didn't matter, and gone were the days of all that dreadful rehearsing in the mirror of the sort of thing to talk to girls about, which never worked anyway, not even when you remembered what it was you had been rehearsing and got the words in the right order.

We learnt that we could make each other laugh. That was a real breakthrough. I had never imagined actually being able to laugh in her presence, being used only to staring at her in open-mouthed, reverential, idiotic silence and giving her a good view of my tonsils. We learnt that we liked much the same sort of films and much the same sort of music and read the same sort of books and liked the same teachers and the same subjects and hated the same teachers and the same subjects, and we both agreed that it was invariably the teachers' fault and that made us laugh, and we had this and that to say about our parents and that just got us rolling round the carpet laughing our heads off, with the tiny trembling kitten trying its steps out and strutting its stuff right there in the middle. It took us ages to decide on a name for it, an endless, endless discussion which seemed to go on in some idyllic Neverland where there was only me and her and the kitten and ice lollies from the freezer, and sometimes our hands would meet, and tingle, and draw back, charmed and startled, as we both decided to caress it at the same time. I can still remember the incredible warmth of that small hand and its unbelievably slim, spotless, gleaming fingernails with the most impossibly candid half-moons at the quick.

And that kitten was there, right in the middle, when I kissed a girl (I mean, really kissed a girl) for the first time in my life and it was like kissing the first days of summer, their crisp, early mornings and their long, warm, humming evenings under the pulsating, lucid brightness of a myriad of splendid stars, and it was one of the most monumental moments in my existence and something that time has never managed to steal or even erode in the least, something I have never quite been able to let go of, and a part of me is still lost in that kiss and a part of me is still with her, and will always be with her, through the years and oceans that divide us.

Just an example, as I said before, of what cats, even tiny little cats, can do when they put their minds to it.

6

A little history (2)
Cats in the ancient world

Cats did not have a good press in the ancient world. Dogs appear in Mesopotamian and Persian art, and one dog, at least, appears in quite an important role in the Mahabharata, one of the great ancient epics of India, just as Argus, the symbol of canine fidelity, appears in Homer's *Odyssey*. We are not informed as to whether Ulysses or Arjuna and his brothers also had cats: if they had, the epics are silent on them. But perhaps we should not read too much into this as it may just mean they were out mousing most of the time, and sagaciously keeping well away from the dogs (and the poets). There is the feeling that dogs in

26

many ancient cultures were considered, at any rate in part, unclean animals, much as they are in the more recent Islamic tradition, but at least they were present in their art – sometimes, as we have just seen, playing quite an important and dignified role. Cats, on the other hand, had to keep their heads down and had a very low profile. In historical terms, cats do appear in the Vedas, ancient Indian Sanskrit texts, but we cannot say that they are treated with much respect.

It was the Egyptians who first gave cats an important, starring role in their lives and culture – a role that was far more significant than any that the dogs, with all their upper-class huntin', shootin' and fishin' kudos, ever enjoyed. The Egyptians, who clearly appreciated such abstract characteristics as inscrutability and poise, elegance and introspection, found precisely these features in their cats, as we still do today, and consequently elevated them to a semi-divine status. When their cats died, they went into periods of mourning and stuffed them and mummified them and everything, although duty obliges me to say that they did much the same thing with crocodiles – they did not, it seems, show that much discrimination in the sort of things they wanted to stuff and mummify (it seems even the occasional duck was involved). Maybe they were scared of crocodiles and wanted to keep them happy so that they wouldn't slyly creep in when darkness fell and gobble them up, the sort of thing that has always given crocodiles a bad name.

However, one thing is certain: the Egyptians are the only people of the ancient world who included the cat in their pantheon of divinities, and their modern-day descendants have every right to be proud of them. This is something that distinguishes them and makes them stand out from other peoples, to say nothing of their pyramids and hieroglyphics and statues and things. It was a dignity which they never accorded to the canines, who for the Egyptians, too, it seems, smacked of the unclean.

In my opinion, it was this deifying of cats by the Egyptians which was the original cause of the long feud – or, let us be honest, inexpiable war – raging between cats and dogs. Before this event, cats were quite happy to keep their time-honoured low profile, skulking modestly in corners and courtyards, while the dogs hogged the limelight and got all the best grub because they were supposed to be so good as hunting partners and so good as guards. Then, suddenly, the cats got promoted to godlike status for some incomprehensible reason and that must have made the dogs so cheesed off they could spit. One can just imagine the sort of talk that went on round the kennels and stables and lamp-posts when that hit the airwaves:

'What? That little sod up there a god? No way!'

'I knew him as a kitten – it makes you spit!'

Really, one cannot blame the dogs, but anyway that was it. From then on, cats and dogs have been sworn enemies, and although there is fraternisation and there are truces and Mothers For Peace and grey lines and anomalous friendships and lifelong bonds between kittens and puppies whose mothers shared childbirth in the very same basket and all that sort of thing, it seems unhappily certain that this multimillenniary *status quo* is likely to endure in perpetuity. It is also true, to be fair to all, that dogs, generally speaking, do not get on very well with crocodiles either, but there may be different reasons for this, such as the fact that crocodiles, very unkindly and quite ignorantly, tend to consider dogs in terms of protein value more than anything else and, frankly, nobody, not even the lowliest creature, really likes to be thought of as somebody else's dinner. Anyway, that problem at least has not been handed on to us, because we don't tend to keep crocodiles as pets. Not yet, at any rate. And this, I might add, is very wise of us. Given their reputation.

Anyway, once they got made gods, those cats in Egypt must have had a field day. They came out of the closet and strutted their stuff and paraded round the place showing off and rolling about and revelling in the fact that everyone was looking at them and pointing at them and saying, 'It's him, it's him! Quick, get his autograph!' and making little toy figures of them and feeding them off the fat of the land and having slaves to play with them all day and all night too if they wanted, tossing corks and swinging balls of wool, and they could even scratch them too if they felt like it and woe betide any slave that took it badly. Then they would have to sit for the sculptors and artists and get themselves immortalised in stone in all their finery, piercing included – nose, ears and sundry other parts of the body. And outside the door the dogs would all be slouching around sullen and whining and going 'Why him?' under their breath and refusing their dinners.

7
Cat-owners and their cats

People react very positively to individual peculiarities and idiosyncrasies in their cats. This is something that the cats themselves got wise to a very long, long time ago, and, being the smart animals they are, learnt to exploit to the full. These things, to an outsider, are often banal and superficial in the extreme but, as we well know, beauty is in the eye of the beholder. What for one person is pedestrian or commonplace or downright idiotic, for another is something that simply creases you with laughter or renders you speechless with amazement and admiration.

Some people will boast that their cat relieves himself in the toilet, just as a human being does, and will communicate this fact to their guests as a sign of unusual genius, placing their animal in much the same category as Einstein or Shakespeare or something. They will be totally blind to the simple and obvious fact that some of their listeners might find such an idea quite nauseating, and will be mentally putting on their overcoats then and there, secretly vowing never to set foot in their bathroom, or indeed even their house once they are safely out of it, ever again.

Others will claim that their cats can observe precise timetables: 'You know, he always turns up for his dindins at seven-thirty precisely and woe betide us if we're not there' – although, to be honest, when I've been present at such a specific time it has always, funnily enough, just happened to be the one time he's been late.

Yet others will delight in, and widely publish, the fact that their cat will only eat at (that is, it pains me to say, *on*) the dinner table, when the rest of the family are having lunch, crazily indifferent to the fact that, for many people, the mere idea of a cat on or even around the dinner table at mealtimes is just revolting. People will proudly display small, shabby toys that their cats kick around the room and play with, almost as if they were sacred relics or museum pieces of immense value. Visitors, when confronted with such rarities, are often totally at a loss as to what to say, and are also burdened by the growing suspicion, not unaccompanied by fear, that their hosts are at least a little mad, something which tends to inhibit conversational flow and to render ordinary social intercourse somewhat fraught.

Cat-owners vie with each other over their cats' dietary proclivities, along the lines of:

'My cat eats pasta.'

'Mine eats roast potatoes.'

'That's nothing, I used to have one that ate pencils!'

'Well, mine ate a wasp and it stung him in the windpipe.'

And the duels and one-upmanship go on and on, the

claims becoming ever more improbable and ever more impossible. Marvels of taste are heaped on the backs of the various long-suffering animals who have heard it all before, poor things, oh, how many times, and are just sitting there staring at nothing and wondering when it is all going to end.

Cat-owners' stories, I am sorry to say, have much in common with fishermen's tales or old sailors' yarns – truth very much takes a back seat. How the poor creatures must blush under their fur and cringe, cowering under the table or behind the sofa, when they have to listen to their most recondite dietary and other bodily secrets aired in public by their unfeeling families. One can only imagine the kind of horrible revenge they would take if only they could talk.

Then there are the near-epic feats of intelligence or the breathtaking exhibitions of gymnastic excellence demonstrated by so many cats – at least according to their owners, since the sad fact is that so many of these incredible events seem to take place only in the presence of the owners themselves and their nearest and dearest, and are seldom, if ever, reliably witnessed by disinterested outsiders.

Let me be completely honest here. With all the respect I have for cats; with all the infinite belief, and willingness to believe, that I have in their abilities and their potential; with all the goodwill I hold towards them – well, some of these stories make even the fishermen's most outrageous hyperbole pale into the banal, sublunary realm of the possible.

'Oh, do you know what that cat did yesterday?' says one, pointing at a still small heap in the corner that looks, if anything, like a superannuated feather duster with eyes. 'He was after that blackbird in the drive and took a running leap and jumped right over the car and landed practically on top of the blackbird . . . No, of course he didn't catch it! He doesn't really want to . . .' And the feather duster with eyes stretches and yawns in his corner and flashes the visitor a sardonic glance and sticks out his hairy tongue and relapses back into slumber, looking for all the world as if he doesn't have the energy to crawl across to the kitchen for his grub, never mind jump over cars, running leap or not. But woe betide you if you even twitch an eyebrow – or the hair of an eyebrow – in disbelief, because that's how blood feuds get started and are carried on remorselessly from father to son, down through countless generations, even after the original *casus belli* has faded into the mists of oblivion.

'Oh, my cat can draw back the bolt to get into the shed,' says another, and you wonder quietly to yourself why he can't open padlocks while he's at it, or maybe even a can of cat-food with the tin-opener. Then you could teach him how to go shopping for himself and he'd be completely self-sufficient and that way you could go on holiday with an easy mind.

'Mine can change channel with the remote control,' says another, in a voice thrilled with wonder. 'He's got his favourite programmes, you know,' when the real truth of the matter is that maybe, just once, that cat simply happened to land on the remote control when he was jumping up for his usual snooze on the sofa and the whole thing got transmogrified, through a process of retelling, and with nothing lost in the retelling, into the stuff of myth and legend. Of course, this is only a beginning. By the time that story has worn itself out, not only does that cat know how to use the remote control, but he can change the batteries in it, too, getting the polarisation right, and can find the right channels and laughs at the sit-coms and has his favourite spots and hisses when the dogs come on. There is, after all, no stopping the exponential growth of a myth: that's what a great deal of human civilisation is all about.

Then there are all those common-or-garden cats who can answer the phone. There are so many of those around that they have basically become a bore.

Still, I must say that, though I have heard of lots of them who can do it, I have never heard one actually do it. I have sometimes rung the numbers of those who boast that their cats can do it, both when I knew they were in (so they could show their cats off) and, slyly, when I knew they were out (so the cats could answer for themselves without being inhibited by the presence of their owners), just to see, and it has never happened to me, so scepticism, I am afraid, does creep in.

Nor should we overlook all the cats who love Elvis. I have even known of a cat who *was* Elvis, though I must admit he never sang for me.

Then, of course, there are all the cats who can't. Just as there are some cat-owners who swell with pride as they try to pass off their cats as a feline genius, so there are those who exult at the sheer extent of their cats' perceived stupidity. The idea seems to be fairly simple: if you haven't got the most superlatively intelligent cat in feline history, then you have to have the most idiotic. Either extreme, it seems, is, in any case, a distinction and something to boast about. The important thing for such owners is that their cat must not be mediocre but have something, either positive or negative, that makes it stand out.

Many cats who are, in my experience, perfectly

run-of-the-mill and normal, and quite happy to be so, must curl up in mortification in their cosy baskets by the fire and blush and wish they were dead as they hear their owners bragging to perfect strangers (who are probably dog-lovers anyway and not in the least interested, or already *a priori* convinced of the essential stupidity of cats) about the latest clamorous example of their mental subnormality. Do these owners think their cats have no feelings? Do they think they like being passed off as thick?

'. . . No, he's not a Manx, actually – he went out on a limb after a sparrow and fell out of the tree, and the paperboy on his bike went and ran over his tail, and we had to have it amputated. Looks a scream, doesn't he?'

Then there's, 'Look at him – went and shut himself in the washing machine, didn't he! We only realised it after a few minutes when Jenny saw him starting to spin . . .'

All I can say is, there may well be stupid cats, just as there are the less intellectually outstanding exemplars in all species – and while we are on the subject, a genuinely stupid rabbit is something to see: they are rare but they exist, and they are worth travelling miles for. But, as I believe many thinkers far profounder than myself have pointed out, there is nothing else on the face of the planet to beat a really stupid human being when he (or she, for I am nothing if not politically correct) really puts his or her 'mind', for want of a better word, to it.

8
The cat's year: winter

Winter affects different cats in different ways. For the average feline, it is fair to define this season as a period of rest and reflection. But just as there are average cats, so there are also cats on both extremes. There are cats who plunge into almost total hibernation and are never seen from the first day of winter to the first day of spring. God only knows when, where and what they eat, though they never get any thinner, but certainly nobody actually sees them do it. One theory is that they lie doggo, wait until there's no one around, then creep out and pinch something from the larder, drag it back to their basket or lair or wherever it is they are hibernating, and slyly consume it under the covers. Another is that they lie in wait for a passing mouse or other snack-size rodent, then grab it when it arrives and gobble it down. It seems that such cats enjoy doing things this way because it gives them an enigmatic, inscrutable air, an aura of profound mystery, and gets them discussed with curiosity, perplexity and awe; that's the sort of thing that kind of cat really goes in for. It is suggested that cats of this type originally came from a large litter and were pretty well neglected by their mothers and siblings, and so spend the rest of their lives hungry for attention and love and are constantly seeking to create a sensation and get themselves talked about.

Then there are the semi-hibernators. These are usually elderly cats who spend most of the winter in their baskets or, if they can get away with it, on other people's beds, occasionally getting up and crawling wearily and painfully across the floor, with a pathetic expression on their faces and long sorrowful yawns, to their feeding dish. They make a great show of weariness and discomfort as they creep towards their food, making it clear to whom it may concern that they are on their last legs and that this may well be the last meal they will ever enjoy in this world so why don't we try a little harder to make it a bit more savoury just for once.

There is, of course, method to all this. Everyone goes, 'Oh, look at the poor old thing! He's on his last legs and this may well be the last meal he will ever enjoy in this world so why don't we try a little harder to make it a bit more savoury just for once?' Enough said. And he gets patted and fussed over and caressed and hugged and above all fed fed fed with precious titbits, and all sorts of expensive foodstuffs get brought in for the poor old thing, and the whole winter is one long Christmas for him and he tries his hardest to prolong it well into spring. Cats of this category (and they are by no means only the old ones – with the younger ones the refrain is along the lines of, 'Poor *little* thing, he's not used to the cold,' and they get crammed with grub too) get very fat in this period, and have quite a job working it off when the warmer weather comes. But no doubt they would all say it's worth it.

On the other extreme there are the hyper-active cats.

These would never even dream of wasting a whole season flopping around snoozing and stuffing themselves. Life, for them, is for living, and the mere idea of hibernating or semi-hibernating is to be dismissed with the most absolute derision and contempt. That's for lazy fatties and fogies and guzzlers. They view the winter with particular regard especially since, as we have noted, so many cats tend to stay in and lounge about and stuff themselves and dream about the summer and never set foot out of doors for the entire period. This means that the external world is at the disposal of these active cats and at their command, and they do not run the risk of getting themselves beaten up by the local tough cats, something so monotonously normal in the other seasons.

In many ways, it is these, and not the slobs and gluttons, who are the happiest cats of the season. If they do not mind a bit of wind and rain and snow – some cats actually enjoy the variability of the weather and there are even some who love the snow – then the whole world is their playground.

One of my cats, whose name is Clovis, loves the winter more than any other season. He is also a cat who enjoys getting dirty and staying dirty, the dirtier the better, and for him the winter is to be savoured especially for this. Most of the time he returns home happy and grubby and dusty and with his fur all ruffled and his muzzle gaily decorated with spider-webs and bits of twig, with maybe the odd dry leaf or two between his claws. He loves crawling into things and through things and under things and brushing against things and smelling things and tasting things and peeing on things and rubbing against things and rolling around in things – piles of autumn leaves, for example, are one of his favourite treats, because you can do so many of the above and so many other creative things with them if you are a cat.

But winter means mud, and mud is what Clovis really likes. Maybe he's got something of the hippo in his genes.

He is always happy when there is something muddy or grubby to do, and he is never more delighted than when he wakes up bright and early of a chill winter morning and the rain is drizzling down implacably and the sky is overcast with grey and the lawn is sodden and the immediate future is a long vista of mud mud mud and a long day's glorious exploration and play and returning home to be towelled dry and scolded in front of the fire and something nice and abundant to eat as he chatters away, reminiscing on his deeds, with us around him just wishing we could understand a word of what he is saying because we know it must be sheer feline poetry. Yes, Clovis is grubby, but he has soul. And anyway, they say Tennyson wasn't over-bothered about personal cleanliness either, and if a Poet Laureate can do it then so can a poetically-inclined cat.

As I have said, for the average feline, winter is a period of rest and reflection. On the extremes, some cats will go into comas and others will have snowball fights or bring out the toboggan or go through the driving snows with kegs of brandy round their necks looking for people to save. But most cats treat winter with a fair amount of diffidence, and seem to be loitering about moodily most of the time, just moseying along until the spring comes back. I have one cat who hangs morosely and miserably around the back door, waiting for the spring to arrive, and he eyes me lugubriously every time I open the door for one reason or another and he sees it isn't there yet. Being of a fundamentally optimistic nature, he occasionally strolls through to the front door, to see if maybe it hasn't arrived there first (my front door faces south), then comes back with a disappointed air and eyes me accusingly, as if it were all my fault. But I just shrug my shoulders and make a face at him, sure of my own innocence, in this matter at any rate. I have absolutely no control of the weather, not even that of my own neighbourhood.

The majority of cats, perhaps, just loiter around like this, idly and sometimes rather moodily waiting for the reappearance of the spring. They belong to that vast number of cats who detest water in any form other than that of a refreshing beverage, and they like to sit on the window-ledges, staring out at the rain or the snow with an air of distant contempt, purring away gently to themselves because they are in the warm and well fed and snug, and think of all those poor homeless cats who have to find shelter where they can and never know where the next meal is coming from or what it is going to be. Yes, winter, for the average cat, is a period of rest and reflection.

9
Kittens

All cats were once kittens. Few experts would disagree with this affirmation. Some cats never forget this simple fact and, in their own small way, continue to be kittens all their lives, dedicating themselves to play, frolic and amusement, and refusing to acknowledge that there is more to life than balls of wool, gaily coloured straws, toy mice, crisps, rubber balls, snacks, string, cream and basic down-to-earth frivolity.

Such cats, even when they live to a ripe old age, somehow manage to retain, evergreen within them, that first careless adoration and wonder and *faith* with which they became conscious of the world around them in the far-off days of their kittenhood, and they never renege on it. They are the pure and free spirits of the feline world and go through their lives charming all who come across them, gay, irresponsible and irresistible. There is one of them here on my desk at this very minute as I write, shamelessly rolling about as he eats a red pencil which is certainly not his property. His name is Rudy.

I never cease to be amazed by kittens. They are so tiny and helpless yet at the same time so gutsy and single-minded and determined, so dead keen to get on with the business of living, practically from the moment they are born. Literally within minutes (and indeed sometimes seconds, and I am not exaggerating) of their leaving the warm, cosy womb, and after a brief and cursory wash given to them by Mum, who clearly has other things on her mind – usually cleaning-up operations or the arrival of yet more kittens – they are already drinking her milk, sucking noisily, their tiny eyes sealed tight shut, their little hairless paws busily pumping away against Mother's paunch, some of them already actually discovering the pleasant and soothing feline art of purring, or the less pleasant art of bawling their tiny heads off in shrill, peremptory squeals when the milk isn't coming along just as the doctor ordered. There can be few things more touching than the sight of the mother cat with her five or six new-born kits laid out in a neat array at her paps, all busy drinking away while she, purring with pride, one complacent eye on her admiring owners, washes each newcomer in turn and presents them, gleaming, fluffy and spotless, to the eyes of the enchanted world.

It can really be a rather traumatic experience being around a mother cat who is having her first batch of kittens. The fact of the matter is that the unhappy creatures have absolutely no idea what is actually happening to them, and haven't a clue as to the sort of thing they are expected to do. I once found myself alone and defenceless in my house when my little grey cat Pixie gave birth to six kittens, to her complete and total surprise and perplexity, to say nothing of mine. I don't think it could have been particularly hard for her, since when the kittens started coming out, one at a time, poor little Pixie simply continued wandering about the house, quite unaware that anything was happening her, and dragging the tiny little things around the place with her, still attached to their umbilical cords.

When she arrived in my study, dragging the first one behind her, I practically panicked. I had absolutely no idea of how to cope, of the sort of things you are meant to do in this kind of situation. I had seen many kittens born, of course, but I had never had an experience quite like this, and I found myself completely at sea, reduced, even if I do say it myself, to a twitching, gibbering mass of nerves which certainly boded no good to the new-borns or their frankly dim-witted mother. I realised one thing, however. I couldn't just follow that poor cat all over the house as she dragged her firstborn around after her, picking up dust and mewing pathetically, with Pixie gazing around her in wide-eyed bewilderment wondering where the funny noise was coming from.

Rather foolishly hoping that, as this was the first time she had had kittens, there might be only one of them, I screwed my courage to the sticking place. I fetched a pair of nail scissors, sterilised them and, crossing my fingers and toes and whatever else I had to cross and gritting my teeth, I snipped through the umbilical cord close to the wriggling, yelling kitten's tiny belly. Bad mistake, of course. The blood just squirted everywhere. 'Oh no!' I thought. 'That's torn it now. I've gone and killed it. It'll bleed to death! Where's my mum when I need her? What'll I do? Help! Help! Help! What'll I do?'

I raced into the bathroom with the soggy, bloody, dusty and, to be honest, rather disgusting kitten. My heart was beating nineteen to the dozen, or whatever the saying is, and my fingers were pressed lightly against the stump of umbilical cord to stop that ghastly bleeding – or squirting, rather. I rinsed the poor little creature with some tepid water, trying to get the water temperature as close as possible to the temperature of the warm, cosy womb that, to judge from its screeches of outraged protest, it was already bitterly regretting having left. I don't really know why I decided on this course of action: maybe it was instinctive, or maybe my reasoning was that, since it was already pretty soggy and grubby anyway, a bit more water would hardly make any serious difference to its destiny.

Perhaps it was beginner's luck, I don't know, but it

paid off. To my eyes miraculously, the bleeding stopped and the tiny thing wriggling in my hand seemed – well, yes, somewhat affronted, but really none the worse for its dramatic introduction to this life and its premature baptism. It was a tough little chap, that one, you could see that almost straight off, and it lay in my hand mewing and muttering – or maybe I should come clean and say cursing and swearing – its blind little face already shoving here and there vigorously in search of something to start sucking at, determined to get stuck into the serious business of living.

'Well,' I thought, 'the thing now is to get it back to its mum and she'll know innately what to do. All I have to do is get this little fellow plugged on to one of her teats and natural instinct and motherly love will do all the rest.' Did it hell. Nature, instinct and motherly love seemed to have abandoned me in my distress, and all my romantic ideals about motherhood and things like that had to be thoroughly revised.

I followed that mother cat up my house and down my house, tears in my eyes, begging, supplicating, exhorting, debasing myself in her eyes and my own as I hoarsely and sorrowfully appealed to her better nature. I made rash, extravagant promises I would never have been able to keep. But my prayers fell on deaf ears. When I think about it now, I cannot blame her. Pixie quite fussily – and, objectively speaking, quite rightly – turned up her small, neat, fastidious grey nose and refused to have anything whatsoever to do with the horrible, scruffy, sodden, disreputable-looking thing I was trying to stick on to her like a burr. I mean, good heavens, Pixie has class. Every time I got her into a corner or against the wall or whatever and moved the kitten gingerly towards her, gibbering incomprehensible rubbish in soft undertones in order to calm her, she would spring softly away with an air of indignation and disgust, giving me a hurt and reproachful look as if I was responsible for the unspeakably horrendous thing I was trying to palm off on her, and would nip off and hide under something where I could no longer get at her without considerable difficulty and discomfort and perspiration and atrocious language.

To make matters worse, it was not simply a question of just one kitten, as I had so fatuously thought, or at least hoped. It was not the end. It was not even the beginning of the end. It was only the end of the beginning. Others started turning up, and I had to follow Pixie up hill and down dale to get at each newcomer with the nail scissors, this time (experience being a great teacher) snipping the umbilical cords a centimetre or so away from the tiny tummy and thus avoiding that dreadful and traumatic haemorrhage experience of Kitten Number 1.

It is, I believe, fortunate that Pixie is a very classy, cool, phlegmatic and unflappable cat – unlike, in my experience, the common run of grey cats who tend to be no better than they should be – and, when all is said and done, she was very little disturbed by either what she must have seen as my mental breakdown and flight into madness, or the arrival of the kittens themselves. She took the whole matter with considerable detachment, as though it were all happening to somebody else and most certainly not to herself. By the time she had finished, however, she had actually produced six healthy, howling kits in the space of about forty minutes, and throughout this period – to their great indignation, let it be said – she did not show even the slightest curiosity regarding them, or the slightest inclination to feed them or to have anything else to do with them. Nor can one really hold it against her: I mean, nobody had actually told her that when you do certain things certain *results* ensue. It is not only the human race that needs a bit of sex education and sapient briefing on the birds and bees. It would do no harm to cats either. Or to monkeys. And we are told that rabbits are even worse.

After about an hour of terrible suffering I had torn all my hair out in tufts and chunks and I was at my wits' end. I was not actually taking drugs, hard or soft, but I suppose that was only because there were no drugs, hard or soft, around to take. But I was talking to myself, which, the experts tell us, is a very bad sign, and I was hollow-eyed, red-nosed and the ghost of my former self. These, too, are bad signs. I had all the symptoms. I do not know what I had all the symptoms of, but I had them, and it was probably something chronic and life-threatening. When I saw myself in the mirror, in the shadowy gloom of the downstairs toilet where the light-bulbs always fused and large spiders often stalked by night, I screamed and took fright. The human mind was not designed to experience certain things: I was busy experiencing some of them, and I was not enjoying it. And I was alone, alone, all, all alone, alone on a wide, wide sea. Of kittens. There was I with half a dozen of them, mewling away (and it is hard to believe how sturdily a single new-born kitten can mewl when he really wants to let rip, so just imagine a small choir of them) all busily ordering their first meal, and the mother with no idea, not an inkling, that she was, as far as

Nature is concerned, an important part of the feeding process. I had really no idea of what to do, and I genuinely began to believe that all the kittens would die and there was absolutely nothing I could do to save them.

However, Nature is smart. Nature knows one more than the Devil. Nature has her little tricks. And the process of evolution is not billions of years old for nothing. It, too, has learnt the odd thing here and there, what with all that branching out and everything. The simple fact of the matter is that, having given birth to a batch of pretty hefty offspring, Pixie was quite exhausted – to put it vulgarly, but perhaps more aptly, she was knackered – and, after a while, she simply collapsed. At that point, I was able to settle her on to a nice clean cushion inside the cat-carrier, where, quite calmly and collectedly, as though absolutely nothing untoward had happened, she began to take a gentle snooze. And it was at this point that my natural cunning slipped into gear. Once I saw that she had dozed off, I took the first-born kitten, judging that he would be practically maddened with hunger by now, and, calmly, gradually, slowly, carefully and slyly, while at the same time (naturally) with fixed staring eyes and giggling crazily, I edged him into the little cage and towards the nearest nipple

I could distinguish in what the artists like to call the penumbra. It worked a treat. There was no stopping that kitten. He didn't even bother waiting to put on a bib. He just got stuck in there, and then like the Mississippi he just went rolling along. As soon as he got a hold on that nipple he stuck on to it like a very determined little limpet and began to guzzle like a true gourmet.

Half-drugged with sleep, Pixie lazily opened one of her eyes, glanced downwards and the odd whisker began to twitch slowly. If I could have read her thoughts I would have said that what she was thinking was, 'How very curious. A kitten of all things, and it's stuck to one of my teats! Now where on earth did that little chap come from?' And then, suddenly, Nature just switched to play and the inevitable kicked into gear. The purring started. The noisy sucking noises started. Then Pixie, with infinite, dreamy grace, lowered her head and out came her little pink tongue, and the washing sounds started. There, suddenly, she was, tidying up her soggy first-born like an expert.

I would have jumped up and down, of course, and hollered for sheer joy and relief and tap-danced and broken into song and done some rebel yells and played the bagpipes and the Hawaiian guitar and trotted out the canapés and popped the champagne and uncorked the single malt and loudly and raucously phoned for a home-delivery pizza or a Chinese or both and had myself a one-man party, but I reasoned that it would be better not to if I didn't want to scare the new mother into fits. There are certain things one shouldn't do at the bedside of a new mother and one of them is all those things I wanted to do. So I didn't.

I took it cool. I hung on to my *sang-froid* and I nursed that cunning streak of mine. Taking advantage of Pixie's state of post-puerperal distraction – it was deceitful and wrong, I admit, but I did it – I slowly slipped another kitten into the cat-carrier and popped it on to another spare nipple, then another, then another, then another (Pixie has no shortage of good nipples) and then, suddenly, it was done. All the kittens were safely parked, and their proud young mother, stars in her eyes, was gazing happily, and a bit snootily, up towards me between bouts of conscientious, and pretty professional, washing operations with an expression that, inadequately translated, meant roughly, 'Now haven't I been a clever girl? Six lovely kittens, No fuss, No bother. Now what do you say to that?'

'All right, Pixie baby,' I said in a low voice, stroking her soft grey fur and gazing into her sweet, shining eyes, 'that's the way, great stuff. Super. You're the tops,' and staggered off down the pub for a couple of pints and left her to it.

10
The cat's year: spring

April with his showers sweet is a great month if you are a cat. This is because most self-respecting cats will have spent much of the winter in an apparent state of semi-hibernation, keeping as close to the fire as possible, maybe because they are afraid someone will run away with it or possibly just because they are on the look-out for Santa. But when the small fowls start making melody, they realise that it is time for them, too, to be out and about, if for nothing else then maybe just to collar some of those rowdy little feathered friends out there and show them a hard time and make them sing a different sort of tune. And they emerge blinking from their basket by the fire, or from the warm cushion next to the stove, or from their own special, rather hairy pillow-case in the airing cupboard, or from their shady nook next to the boiler, and they stretch their forelegs forward as far as they will go and the rest of their bodies backwards and their tails and bottoms high into the air and out comes a fantastic great yawn that seems to go on and on and on for ever, and they shake themselves and then it's straight out the door to see how the outside world has been managing things without them.

They stop briefly on the patio and give a suspicious lengthy olfactory once-over to the drainpipe and the walls and the fence and the odd tree or so, just to make sure no lout of a dog has been getting into their garden and peeing. Such things have actually happened, other winters, when they have been busy sleeping, and there's nothing, but nothing, gets them more annoyed. Then there is the quick run up and down the yard, the quick twist, the quick agile leap up into the air, the odd yell and yodel, just to clear the throat and make sure the legs and lungs and tonsils and all the rest of the kit are still working all right after their long period of disuse and neglect. Then comes the time of meditation, introspection and reflection, a long, rapt period of immobility, the only sign of life being in their twitching whiskers or the tips of their searching noses, interrogating the crisp, early spring air for new smells, new sensations, new emotions, new promises, new adventures.

It is in the springtime that the ancient lineage of the cat becomes most evident, even if there are no longer rain forests or jungles or primeval savannahs for him to roam about in. We see him respond in an almost mystical manner to the inviting caresses of the sun, alert to every manifestation of the living earth, the clouds, the breezes, the droning insects, the rustling of the trees, the small sounds in the grass. As he looks around, ecstatic, totally entranced, we feel instinctively that the one thought pulsating through his mind is something like: 'This is all so alive and it's all mine.' The human being, the fond cat-owner, may, of course, feel a passing twinge of sadness as he realises that, wherever his beloved pet's thoughts are, they are very far away from him, deep in some arboreal dream that he has nurtured in his genes since the distant beginnings of things. But if he is of a sensitive nature, he may also feel a profound sympathy, even empathy, with his small friend, and some atavistic part of him, too, may hark yearning back to a time when forests were forests and people and animals were, for better or worse, so much closer, so much part of the same world, and our ancestors painted pictures of the animals they loved and hunted on the sooty walls of their caves and the windswept sides of their sacred mountains.

Maybe our cats, in these early days of the spring, can teach us to look straight up into the clouds and the blue sky again with that same sense of wonder that our forebears felt for so many thousands of generations, before we became so worldly-wise and civilised and convinced ourselves that we knew it all, and ended up just alienated and tired and with jaded palates and no longer really at ease with our world. There is considerable wisdom to be gleaned from the observation of cats, especially if we're sensible enough to be able to do it with a spirit of humility, and are still able to see the world in a grain of sand and heaven in a wild flower.

A fly comes buzzing by. When that happens, any cat worth his salt will leap up and try his luck. Ours does, and misses because he is out of practice. But what the heck – there will be plenty more game around, much more respectable, too, than any tacky old fly. Now he has other things on his mind. He wonders how the big dog down the road is getting on. Maybe he'll pop round and see, prance around a bit, stir it up, get it yelling and barking and then sneak off, and with a bit of luck it'll get a good scolding, maybe even a smack. And then there are all the other cats of the neighbourhood to be visited. Hope they're all right, got through the winter okay, no sudden diseases out of the blue, no old-age collapses, no singed fur from sparks from the fire, no milk floats and similar. But before starting off on his rounds maybe it's a good idea to make sure he's looking his best – never know who you might meet. Wouldn't be a good idea to be seen wandering around like some sort of feline tramp, some of the cats round here being so fussy and oh-my-oh-my – 'fastidious', maybe, is the right word, or 'stuck-up' is even better.

So he checks his paws to make sure they're clean. It would be dreadful, really dreadful, to stroll up to an old pal and suddenly find you've got – well, nameless things of uncertain provenance stuck to your claws or between your toes. Then maybe a good kick up a bit behind him just to make sure the back paws are in order too. Then he sits down, and a quick, discreet sniff here and there, a quick lick where necessary, special care for the armpits and the (shall we say) upper-tail zone, and any worrying doubts with regard to body odour are laid to rest. Then a spot of manicure – across to the nearest tree or post or maybe just somebody's nice shiny gate (e.g. mine) and a good vigorous scratching, and hey presto! the perfect set of claws, you won't find a better between here and Hollywood.

Then there is the small but lively – it is spring for them too, poor dears, after all – question of fleas. Well, a quick scratch here and a quick scratch there – my, what a marvellous set of claws, even if I do say so myself – and a quick bite here and a nibble there and another one just there, aah! and the flea problem is temporarily solved. Then off we go, strutting, out (or rather under) the gate and down the road, proud as a peacock, whiskers all a-bristle, feelers twitching, tail erect, and it's 'Come on, world, we're back on the beat! Show us what you've got!'

And it always does, of course. That's its job. Indeed, it sometimes really does seem that the world was just made for cats.

'Well, hello hello hello!' Meeting another cat he hasn't seen since the chill set in. 'Well, well, you've put on the odd kilo or so, haven't you, chum?'

'You're no matchstick yourself, are you? Ha ha.'

'Oh, just the good old winter fat – we'll soon run that off. Where you heading?'

'Actually I was just going up the road to see what's doing.'

'Well, you go up and I'll go down and we'll meet up later and compare notes.'

'Yeah, see you later.'

And off one swaggers in one direction and off one swaggers in the other and 'Oops, a new dog at number thirty-nine.'

And then he finds a small thing crawling across the pavement in front of him and stops to eat it and 'Yuck! What on earth was that? Spit, spit, spit, cough,' and then he slinks rapidly under a hedge because he hears the high-pitched purr of the milk float and he's heard what those things can do and it's better to be safe than sorry and there are children in the garden on the other side and they start going, 'Puss puss puss puss puss puss,' and he feels nice and safe because it's a fine thick hedge with bristles and then one of them has the bright idea of bringing him out a saucer of milk and if there's one thing he'll never refuse it's a nice saucer of milk so he crawls out, stomach close to the ground and ears set back and ready to make a break for it if necessary, and that milk smells *sooo* fresh and cool and a little pink tongue slips out and there's nothing, *nothing* nicer than an unsought treat like this and then a little hand comes out, cautious, cautious, eager and trembling a bit with tiny, incredibly delicate fingers, and starts patting him softly softly and he knows it's all right now and he straightens up and he gets on with the milk and he lets them pat him as much as they want and purrs a bit and miaows a bit and that gets them really pleased and now he's got a nice new spare family to visit any time he feels like a little snack or a cuddle or maybe even, if he's lucky, a game with a piece of string or a ball of wool or something and isn't spring great. The milk finished, aaah, saucer spotless, and it's time to get back on the road. A brisk little roll in the grass, paws pedalling the air, just to give the kids a laugh, a little thank-you miaow, polite and finely modulated, because without a bit of manners we might as well be back in the jungle swinging off trees with the lemurs, and it's off again after a quick wash-and-brush-up of the whiskers. He can't be wandering around the streets with milk all over his face, just wouldn't look right. After all, he's not a kitten, is he?

And so the spring and the cats come out together, in perfect amity and harmony. The young green shoots have started popping out and he has a quick chew of this one and a quick nibble of that one and a quick roll over these ones and a quick scrabble round those ones. And some of them taste all right and some of them taste ghastly, but that's what spring's all about: you just never know what you'll get, and just as well too, because that would spoil the surprise. The showers sweet start coming down and he laps at the fresh, earthy water in the puddles, thinking he has never tasted anything quite so good, quite so *invigorating* – the taste of life itself. He has a try for some of the small fowls making melody, but they're just a bit too smart for him, full of all the zest and energy of spring. Still, who cares? He only goes after them because it's in his blood, not because he really wants to harm them, and he's not even hungry, and anyway there's nothing worse than the stomach-ache from a handful of feathers. He meets up with old acquaintances and makes new friends. He renews his association with car tyres and lamp-posts – dreadful smell of dog – with fences and hedges and vacant plots and empty houses and building sites and gardens and shed roofs and low walls and narrow lanes and ditches, and he climbs a few trees just to see the view from up there, and the fat melts off him, miraculously, as if it had never been there at all, and he starts shedding all his excess winter fur and suddenly he's slim and sinuous and clean-limbed and healthy and alert and full of beans and he becomes one with the spring, practically the spirit of the spring itself, all energy and hope and curiosity, and everything is all so familiar yet at the same time so mysterious.

11
Remembering The Fiend

I have had many cats, and it is fair to say I have loved most of them. Not all of them, I must admit, but most of them. For years I had, to be honest, a thoroughly unlikable one – that's certainly what all the neighbours said, and I must admit I totally agreed with them, at least at the beginning. I half-had her, to be more accurate, because she spent far more time away from us than actually at our home, living a vagrant, wandering, gypsy sort of life, turning up every so often for a bite to eat and a snooze by the fire when it was cold, then off out again on her adventures. No, I cannot say that I liked her, but I did tolerate her. She was small and taut and tense,

70

a hostile, spitting bundle of nerves whenever you tried to stroke her, definitely not the sort of cat that jumps into your lap for a cuddle and a crisp or a bit of salty biscuit. It was not very respectful, I know, but we used to call her The Fiend, and she was basically our yardstick when we wanted to run down some or other of our neighbours – 'that old Mrs Short across the road there, she's worse than The Fiend', that sort of thing.

She was never formally introduced to us, as it were. She was just there one morning, joining the crowd of cats round the big blue plastic washing-bowl that we then used for their meals, and indeed, since she was rather a small cat, we would hardly have noticed her at all in the throng save for the fact that she had extremely distinctive markings – what looked like a long fishbone, in black, down a honey-coloured back. She was not a beauty: her peculiar, rather off-putting coat was accompanied by wicked little eyes and a small, pinched, scowling face, wary, malevolent and threatening, exuding vibes of the type, 'You keep your distance, you, or I'll rip your bloody eyes out,' and you somehow didn't want to put her to the test. She was the sort of cat that looked as though she meant business, and I've learnt from experience that it's better to give cats that look as though they mean business a wide berth, because they usually do mean business. Especially the she-cats because, unquestionably here, the female of the species is deadlier than the male. However, it never occurred to any of us to chase her away, even though my irate neighbour described her all in one breath as a *nastybad-temperedlittlebitch* when he caught her overturning his milk to get at the cream and refused to believe she wasn't one of my large and growing extended feline family. If she wanted to turn up at feeding-time and have a few mouthfuls in a safe and friendly environment then that was all right by us. As I say and repeat, I can't say that any of us actually liked her, but a bit of charity, surely, isn't just for those you like.

Anyway, as the French say, *tout comprendre c'est tout pardonner*. While not being actually pleasant to see, The Fiend's markings were most certainly highly distinctive. She was the sort of cat that you could pick out from a thousand, and she would have been absolutely hopeless as a criminal because she would have stuck out like a sore thumb in any identity parade. One day, as she was strolling across our garden to grab a bit of grub, I noticed two rather tough-looking youngsters stop and start loitering round our gate, staring across at her. 'It's 'er,' they were saying, 'yeah, that's 'er all right,' clearly recognising her.

My curiosity aroused, I walked across to them. 'Know that cat?' I asked.

'Yeah, it's my sister's, or used to be,' said one of the boys, still staring at The Fiend. 'It ran off a couple of years back, an' never came back.'

'Oh?' I said, being myself no stranger to the heartbreak of The Cat That Went Away. 'Then maybe your sister'd be happy to have it back. It's not that the cat lives here, you know, she just pops in every so often for a bite to eat and a bit of company. I don't know where she lives now. I'll be happy to give you a hand if you want to take her back home with you.'

'Nah, s'all right,' the boy said. 'My sister doesn't even live with us any more. She's gone to work in Birmingham.'

'Anyway,' the other boy put in, with a rather nasty little grin, 'I don't think that cat would like to come back round our way again.'

'Oh?' I said again, and I didn't really like his expression. 'Why's that?'

'The lads round our way,' he said, and I was sure from something in his expression that in fact these two little hard cases had also been part of it, 'used to play football with her.' He gave a tough, uneasy little guffaw. 'She was the football.'

As I turned back towards the house I saw The Fiend crouched, or rather bundled, down, tense, vicious, ferocious, under a garden chair, gazing with blazing, vengeful eyes towards the backs of the two disappearing youngsters. Maybe she hadn't seen them for two years, but cats, like elephants, never forget certain things, especially things like kindness and things like ill treatment. 'Puss puss puss puss puss,' I said in as gentle and tranquillising a tone as I could, 'come and have some grub and forget those two.' But she seemed to have lost her appetite and wandered off slowly and dismally, her body stooping and dejected, and I didn't see her for quite a few weeks. Then she turned up again and our old, diffident half-friendship was gradually re-established, but I often saw her interrupting her feeding and looking suspiciously towards the fence, as if she feared the reappearance of those two unlovely figures from a nightmare past. We found a new, kinder, more flattering name for her in due course, but though she did, to a certain extent, mellow with time, I would still often look at her and think, inside myself, 'What a little fiend!' and I kept myself at a respectful distance. With cats like that, you never know. You just never know.

12

A funeral

There's an old idea around, I don't know who started it but it wouldn't surprise me if it was Shakespeare, that when a writer's got writer's block and is stumped for ideas, the best way out is a good funeral. Not his own, naturally. That would be a bit too – well, final and conclusive, or at least very trying and uncomfortable if he was still alive. No, what I mean is that a funeral is a good thing to write about if the writer has got stuck.

My personal feeling is that it's probably not a bad tip. Indeed, it's a pretty good one if you're writing a novel, or for the theatre or, of course, if you're a poet. Serious poets could really enjoy themselves with a funeral. However, it is not advice that I would suggest following in all fields of writing. It is not something that, for example, I would advise the writers of cookery books to feel themselves bound by, nor those who are writing children's books about bunnies and teddies, or manuals for the use of electro-domestic appliances. The important thing, as in so many aspects of life, is to know the right place and the right time for things, and I am certainly not the first person to say this as I am reliably informed that the Bible itself also says it, and better than me, too.

But *revenons à nos moutons*, as the French say (or, in our context, maybe *revenons à nos chats* works better), with a question. Is it all right to bring funerals into a book about cats? It is a bit of dilemma, I admit. But I can offer at least a couple of things in favour of the idea: in the first place, I have got writer's cramp, or block, or whatever they call it, so you readers might as well make up your minds: either you get a funeral or you get no rest of the book, and it's still more or less in mid-air at the moment (as, all right, I am the first to admit). Then there is the other very valid point, in my opinion, that cats do die, whether they like it or not, just like every other life form, and it's only fair to talk about what we do with them when this unhappy event takes place. Otherwise, who knows what sort of ideas people would get into their heads?

The Egyptians used to mummify theirs, as I have already observed, and tens of thousands of cat mummies, all scrupulously embalmed and everything, have been found by archaeologists all over ancient Egyptian sites. Crocodiles, as I have also said, received much the same treatment, and often their mummified bodies were stuffed with old papyrus documents – whole books sometimes, up the back passage I am sorry to say, and I hope they diligently checked the poor creatures were dead and everything first. Cats, being smaller, did not have to undergo quite the same process.

I have buried no crocodiles, but I have, sad to say, buried many cats, though I have embalmed and mummified none. Nor have I stuffed any with priceless papyrus documents, having too much respect both for cats and for priceless papyrus documents. I have had cats that have lived to a good old age. I have had cats that have lived to a ripe old age. And I have had one cat that lived to a grand old age, and by that I mean considerably over twenty. That was my poor old Tibby, the great-great-great-great grandmother of many of my present cats and one of the glories of nature.

In her younger days, her salad days as the saying goes, Tibby was a real *femme fatale*. Without disrespect to her memory, it is only fair to say that she was inordinately fond of what used to be called sexual union, and, to use another obsolete phrase much loved by our grandparents, she regularly 'got into trouble'. Not that this bothered her over-much: she was a free spirit, and she knew what she liked and she went for it. Enthusiastically. The task of having to find decent homes and careers and futures for the furry and bewhiskered fruits of her sinful ways fell, of course, to me and my family. She herself was happy to reproduce, to go forth and multiply as it were, feed her issue (and, be it said to her credit, feed them abundantly) for the necessary period, and bid them farewell without a tear or a backward glance. For some of my readers a cynical creature, perhaps, but in her way straightforward and honest. At least you knew where you stood with her.

I sometimes, by the way, exercise myself in trying to work out exactly what proportion of my life I have dedicated to finding homes for kittens that I will never see again and that will never as much as say thank you for all my efforts. I usually abandon the exercise in despair. And the fact of the matter is that a large percentage of those very kittens came from one particular source: Tibby.

Imagine two or three clutches (I'm sure that's hens but what the hell, poetic licence can be allowed even in a book about cats) a year, five to six kittens per batch (I'm sure that's bread; ditto), for over twenty years. That sure is a lot of kitten. If there is an international prize going for that sort of thing I should most certainly be in the running for it. Several times over. So I'm claiming it, you lot out there. And I hope it's money because I could do with a good holiday. And if the reader is snorting irately and thinking, 'But why didn't you get her doctored, you big eejit?' all I will say is, I meant to, I really *meant* to. It's just that I never really got round to it. You know how these things are.

Years passed. Tibby was a phenomenon of nature, not only in her carnal proclivities but in her ability to withstand the whips and scorns of time with the most incredible vitality and grit. She was well over twenty before she stopped going out and about and settled down to spending long hours dozing in her favourite basket near the fire, surrounded by her multitudinous, chaotic but, I hope, adoring and dutiful posterity. Well, to be completely honest, they did not, regrettably, always treat her with the proper respect due to a Grande Dame of her years, experience and status, but, as we all know, there has always been something – well, spontaneous, not to say downright anarchic, about healthy kittens, especially when they are all got together in a mob.

Then her faculties started failing her. I don't know how long it took for it actually to happen – my impression is that it came on extremely rapidly, literally from one day to the next – but all of a sudden we realised that the poor thing had gone blind. Not just short-sighted, I mean, but blind as the proverbial bat, walking into walls and things, snuffling around helplessly for her food, banging her nose against the table-legs, standing still for long periods of time in the middle of the floor, disorientated and unhappy and scared: the whole works.

It shocked and saddened us all. She had been with us so long, she had always been such a character, so full of life, so full of guts, and here was our poor old cat blind, helpless and powerless, in so many ways just the shadow of everything that she had been.

Naturally, though reluctantly, we had to talk about having her put down. We reasoned that her life had become a burden to her, that she was living a groping, fumbling, terrified life in the dark, unable to defend herself against any threat that should arise, basically trapped inside a nightmare which she could never begin to understand and from which she would never awake again. However, since she seemed, despite her blindness, quite healthy and serene in every other way, and clearly still enjoyed her food and her snoozes, we decided not to take any definitive action. Not to rush things, at any rate. The important thing was to make sure that she felt safe and warm and protected and looked after and had all she needed to eat and to drink, and that she should have no particular reasons for anguish or fear, and then things could take their natural course.

Things did take their natural course. She was, as I have said, a very old cat and certain other faculties began to fail her. She became incontinent, peeing (and peeing abundantly) wherever the impulse took her, and an old cat's pee here and there around the house is not to be confounded, and never will be confounded, with eau de Cologne. She developed dental problems and most of her teeth went – not that she really needed them, because we were giving her pretty soft, pappy stuff to eat, anyway, that she didn't need to chew. Then we realised after a bit that not only was she blind, but that she had gone deaf as well. That was another nasty shock for us. When she was, as it were, only blind, all we had to do was call her name and she realised it was feeding time and made a bee-line for her bowl, never making the slightest mistake. It was sufficient that we made sure there were no obstacles in her path, and she would make her way to wherever she wanted to go in perfect confidence. But now she was deaf, stone deaf. When we called her, she simply didn't hear us. You could probably have burst a balloon right next to her and she wouldn't have noticed a thing – not that we would have dreamt of trying any such thing. Again, we had to think seriously about having her put to sleep, feeling that this was no life for her. Who knew what went on in her poor old head, in that shut-off, closed, dark and silent world in which she now dwelt? How could she understand what had happened to her, how could her mind come to terms with it? At least you can explain concepts like blindness and deafness to a human being. They might not like it but, at least up to a point, they can understand it, and understanding an affliction is part of the way to coping with it. But how do you explain things like that to cats? We really worried about that. We wondered if she could see a glimmer of anything through those tired, clouded eyes, or hear even the slightest thing, reasoning – perhaps fallaciously, but we were, after all, clutching at straws – that that would have made things a little better for her.

But Nature is a tough baby. Though Tibby had lost two of her senses, she had by no means lost her marbles or her appreciation of the simple things of life. We suddenly realised that though she was, it is true, both deaf and blind, she had not lost her senses of touch and smell, and nor had she lost her sense of taste. When she felt like it, she would get up and go for a little stroll around the house, relying on her whiskers and those feelers that are a cat's eyebrows, and was soon wandering around in perfect tranquillity, almost as if she could see. And when we were putting out the food for the other cats, ladling things out or opening cans and packets and things, she, in her basket, would spring to attention as soon as she caught the odour, and perhaps very very faintly the sound, and would soon be making her slow, methodical but determined way over for her own share, busily tucking in, toothless or not, with satisfied smacking sounds and considerable gusto.

We started buying her some of those expensive little cat meals and feeding her on the sly away from all the other cats, who would have guzzled them down in a trice showing no respect or consideration for the old and infirm, and the unmixed delight with which she slowly and systematically devoured them, without haste, without stress or sass from the others, was a joy to watch. A cat who could still get such pleasure from existence was, we reasoned, by no means an unhappy animal, by no means an animal in pain or distress or haunting a nightmare world (if anything, we were the ones having the nightmares, not her) of terror and anguish. On the contrary, she was one happy cat, far happier (and this is beyond dispute) than so many of the hopeless and abandoned cats dragging out a hungry, melancholy and disease-ridden half-life in so many of our cities. She was being protected and fed and looked after, caressed and cuddled, her every need ministered to, and we genuinely admired her toughness and guts and grit. What more could any cat ask in the twilight of its days?

But, of course, things got worse. One can perhaps, with care and affection, alleviate many of its more negative effects but, let us be honest, there is no cure for old age. Do what you like: once that has really set in there is no way back. The next thing was that poor old Tibby went through a phase of having convulsions, a bit like epileptic seizures, during which she would stagger blindly round the room, howling and banging her poor head against the walls or the furniture. Or she would get into the centre of the room and then start blundering round in a tight obsessive circle, round and round and round, aimlessly, mindlessly, crazily, for ages if we let her – and indeed, it was not that easy to stop her.

That was it, we decided. We didn't know if she was actually in pain or not, but the possibility was there and it was very troubling. Let's call the vet, we said, and we'll see about the injection. It's quite wrong of us to make a poor old animal suffer in this way. And we actually did ring our vet, a man who, in the course of years of painstaking and conscientious and extremely generous and self-sacrificing service to us (I hope he's reading this – thanks, J., for everything) had become a close and very dear friend, both to us and to the cats. But the fact was that it was the holiday period and he was away and had not left a substitute to stand in for him. And although we did try, half-heartedly, to find another couple of vets, we felt that if anyone was going to put old Tibby down it ought to be the vet who had known and cared for her for so many years – so when we got no answer to our phone calls we agreed to wait until he should come back.

I'm so glad we did. Tibby's convulsions recurred, on and off, for four days, and then they stopped just as suddenly as they had come. We don't know why they came, or why they stopped, or why they never happened again in the time remaining to her, but a curious subsequent event may have had something to do with it.

Nor do we know if what happened, what I am about to try and describe, was typical in situations of this nature, or unique. All we do know is that it happened, and that it was something rich and strange, unforgettable and breathtakingly marvellous, something that warmed our lives for quite a while – perhaps, indeed, permanently. There is considerable wisdom to be gleaned from the observation of cats, even when they are old and grey and full of sleep, and nodding by the fire, deaf, blind, incontinent and in their extreme dotage.

It was a short time – a matter of two or three weeks, if I remember rightly – after Tibby had recovered, as it were, from her bout of convulsions. She had settled into a placid, sedate, quasi-invisible lifestyle in which she spent most of her time in her own little basket, just occasionally getting up to walk round and round in her little tight, blind obsessive circles, coming out regularly as clockwork to guzzle down one of her favourite little meals. And a dramatic event happened in our little family of cats.

One of Tibby's descendants, an odd rusty-coloured little creature with peculiar patchwork markings all over her, gave birth to a litter of five kittens. Her name was Garbage, and we gave her that name precisely because of her appearance – viewed from certain angles Garbage looked exactly like a dustbinful of rubbish, and pretty seedy-looking rubbish at that.

The name, by the way, was just right for her. Garbage lived up to it, or maybe she did what she did because she resented having been given such a name in the first place, held it against us and wanted to teach us a lesson. Whatever the justification – and we are only too ready to forgive our cats their little slip-ups – we feel that she should not have done it, and wherever she is now we hope she is thoroughly ashamed of herself. She let herself down, and the entire feline race with her.

One bright morning, Garbage simply walked out on her kittens. Flying in the face of all the rules of nature, cocking a snook at the ancient and honoured instinct of motherhood, totally ignoring all the canons of fair play and correct behaviour, that cat just strolled out into the garden as if she wanted to take a bit of air, gazed around her innocently as if considering the beauty of the morning, gave me one sheepish, guilty look, then did a runner, split for the horizon, and was never seen again from that day to this. It is not, by the way, that there was anything wrong with those kittens – it was a splendid little litter, and she should have been proud of herself instead of sneaking off like that and ratting on her duties as a cat and a mother.

The result, of course, was tragic. I hope Garbage is reading this now, preferably in tears, and realises just how low-down her behaviour was. We know there are great trials and tribulations in being a single mother, but we were all around her, ready to give her all the help and moral support that she needed, and we feel that she should have thought about it and discussed things with one of us or with a friend or perhaps some minister of religion before making her break for freedom. It may well be that now she is sorry for what she did, and what we say is, if Garbage ever turns up again, which is unlikely to say the least, we will let bygones be bygones and have her back. But not for this shall I try to whiten her or pass over the terrible consequences of her desertion of her post. All the kittens – tiny, helpless, charming, mewing little things – died. We did what we could, of course, trying desperately to feed them with improvised teats, with droppers, with syringes, buying expensive milk substitutes and vitamins suggested (without much real hope, I admit) by our vet and our local chemist, staying up all night, taking turns, to do everything possible and imaginable to save them. Mewing piteously, they passed away one by one, tiny pathetic little things introduced briefly into this beautiful world of ours just to die slowly and painfully of malnutrition and dehydration, all before their eyes had even been able to open to give them a brief glimpse of the world they had passed through so rapidly and unhappily.

We had, of course, been used to losing cats for one reason or another. Since we had always had so many of them around, this kind of unhappy experience from time to time was unavoidable. But it had not yet fallen to our lot to have to assist in such a seemingly futile loss of a whole batch of kittens, with us totally impotent and incompetent – human beings, with all our science and knowledge and learning, all our wisdom and experience, quite unable to save a few tiny creatures from a sad and lingering death. It is that sort of experience that really helps to get things into perspective. Humanity may well be a fantastic piece of work: the beauty of the world, the paragon of animals, in action how like an angel, in apprehension how like a god – though I do have my doubts about all this sort of stuff – but, let us be honest, we still have a lot to learn, a heck of a lot to learn, if we cannot save the lives of a handful of kittens.

Ahem, sorry, where was I? Ah yes, as I was saying before I got a bit carried away there, Garbage's kittens simply perished after she abandoned them, in spite of all our efforts to save them. But I should have said all but one, because one of the five actually survived. Surprisingly, perhaps, it was the smallest of the litter and ostensibly the weakest, the kind of kitten that often doesn't last a day even when the mother is still around to look after it. It was a poor little trembling black-and-white critter that, as we later found out, was blind in one eye, possibly as a result of its early deprivations and malnutrition, and, if it is politically correct to say such things of cats, was mentally, somewhat below the average – not excessively so, but certainly no genius. Or, if he was, he's modestly kept it very well hidden for many years. Well, there's nothing wrong with that. Most of us aren't geniuses either, are we?

(I've been putting off the best bit, to create a bit of suspense and get you readers sitting on the edge of your seats and biting your nails, or perhaps those of a nearby loved one – or a nearby stranger, if you are reading on the train – down to the quick. I urge you not to light a cigarette to relieve the tension and stress if you have given up smoking. It would just be a lot of pain and effort thrown away for nothing, and the next time you try to give up it will be all the harder, and you will blame me, and maybe even think about actually suing me, though you cannot deny that I told you not to: it is here, in black and white. And anyway, your torment will soon be over.)

We had this one little kitten left over. How he lasted longer than the others, when he was in such a bad way to start with, we will never know. But he survived. Maybe he was able to absorb the milk and stuff we were desperately giving to his siblings better than they were. Maybe he was just genetically tougher, though, as I have said, he certainly didn't look it. Maybe he was just as stubborn as hell. However, it was soon clear that, in spite of all our efforts, he would go too. He just lay there in his basket snuffling blindly at the air, his little mouth working, his empty, distended belly throbbing, occasionally emitting a long, low, despairing sort of whine. We sat around, sad, sorry and beaten, suffering more for this one than for all the others because he was so small and so wretched and because he was the last one left.

Then the miracle took place. It was towards evening on a warm day in late summer, and I vividly remember the, well, summery sounds outside, all the crickets and stuff, and the warm reddish tinge of the twilight sky. Old Tibby had got out of her basket and was sightlessly picking her way across the room, heading for her dinner, her whiskers, as usual, on the alert for any danger, when suddenly the kitten uttered one of its small, dreadful, dying cries. Deaf as she was, she might just have been able to hear it, being fairly close to the kitten's basket. Anyway something happened to her, inside her.

She stopped in her tracks. She stood there, quite frozen for a few moments, her tatty old claws digging into the carpet, squinting her sightless eyes, sniffing the air, her nose pointing, pointing, and then, suddenly, with no further hesitation, as though her sight had suddenly been restored to her (she was doing it all by smell, of course) she strolled purposefully across to that basket, got in, flopped down on her side, and started purring in a loud – I would even say peremptory – manner which admitted of no contradiction or denial.

Certainly it had its effect on that kitten. It staggered, as far as it was able, up on its tiny, toothpick-thin legs, its little head nodding rhythmically, uncontrollably, and blundered across to Tibby's ancient withered paps. It soon found one of her desiccated old teats and, as it were, plugged itself on and started sucking away.

Tibby purred even louder, and we stood, transfixed in amazement, in wonder, in genuine awe – because, helpless and senile and blind and deaf and toothless and incontinent and whatever else she was, that decrepit old biddy there was actually yielding milk, and to judge from the slurping sounds coming from the kitten, it was high-quality stuff into the bargain, as it well may have been since Tibby was a hearty eater to the end and we had been literally spoiling her with the best stuff on the market.

Tibby had been well on her way out before she found herself landed with this new responsibility, and we firmly believe that rather than hastening her end, as may well have been the case, it actually gave her a reason to keep on going, and a new lease of life. She looked after and mothered that little fellow, fed it and washed it, holding it down firmly with her paws. Being as blind as a bat, she perhaps wasn't washing it as efficiently as she might have done, but so what? Nobody's perfect, and anyway we were around to make up for her defects in this field. It certainly gave her a new interest in life, and after what it had been through the little kitten was quite helpless for a fairly long time, so she had her hands, or paws, quite full in the closing months of her life.

But, of course, although she was as tough as nails she was not immortal. One afternoon, about three months after she had adopted her orphan, we found her dead in her basket, with the kitten staring at her with his one eye, open-mouthed, his head cocked on

one side to see better, unable to understand what was going on, and occasionally prodding at her with a tiny paw. But he was, by then, a fine, plump, well-fed little fellow, glowing with health and energy, and I think Tibby knew, in her last moments, that she had managed to do a sublime job of work in the final phase of her life. She lay there, not like the usual dead cat, whose features often reflect an unhappy and truculent final struggle for life, but as though she had just dropped off to sleep again after a good meal, safe and well and in the presence of those who knew her and cared for her and wished her well.

We cried, of course, although we had known for ages that her end was imminent, because she was our oldest cat and because we had loved her and, above all, because we had been bowled over by the incredible, epic courage and self-sacrifice of her final months. For us, Tibby will always be the archetype of the feline heroine, the archetype of *sheer guts*.

Which brings us at last to our funeral, the original subject of this chapter. We buried her under a solitary wild pear tree in a small and secluded but rather beautiful place we have up in the hills. From time to time, as the years have gone by, she has been joined on the hill by a number of her old friends and acquaintances and descendants. She is not sleeping alone and, I can tell you, the place is a riot of daffodils in the spring.

For some reason, we called the kitten she saved Ronald. And Ronald now has been with us – we would never have dreamt of giving him away, not for all the tea in China – for donkey's years. He is showing all the signs that, barring accidents, he may well yet become another of our Methuselahs, as we call our really elderly cats. It's not bad going for one that had been such a sickly little runt, and one that had been abandoned by his unfeeling mother, and had had to survive the demise of all his siblings into the bargain.

He grew up to be a great big, healthy, muscular, sinewy daredevil of a fellow (I am looking at him right now, sitting on the window-ledge, washing his paws), tough as nails, his debonair, piratical one-eyed flair clearly rendering him irresistible to all the female cats of the area. The tom-cats, too, know a tough guy when they see one, and generally speaking they tend to keep well out of his way. He has had, in consequence, numerous progeny, to use an old-fashioned term.

When we talk it over now, we are all pretty convinced that there must have been some rare property in old Tibby's milk. Maybe not the kind of stuff that goes into the making of an Einstein – as I have said, he's no great brain – but just a good, solid, down-to-earth, no-nonsense, hundred-per-cent cat, reliable and affectionate and a calm blessing in the house, and you can't ask for much better than that. Can you, Ronald? Purr purr purr. *Purr purr*. Cheers!

13
Sounds of summer:
an interlude

There's a big full moon and a cloudless sky
And the wind is low and the stars are bright
And there's a shadow creeping by
On the garden wall on a summer's night

Tiny footsteps through the park
Tiny forms around the gate
Tiny noises in the dark
Tiny shadows crouch and wait

And in the bushes there's a rustle
And something crawls across the grass

And then the garden's all a-bustle
As countless creeping shadows pass

Then one by one the shadows leap
Up on the top of the garden shed
They leap, they bound, they crawl, they creep
They wait until we're all in bed

And then we hear the voice of doom
A long and dreadful, chilling yell
And rising in the brooding gloom
A nightmare from the heart of hell

The cats are in full voice tonight
The repertoire is rich and long
Lined up in the broad moonlight
All the choir breaks into song.

14
The cat's year: summer

All healthy cats love all four seasons, because all healthy cats share an unconquerable love of life that is only incidentally influenced by atmospheric conditions. When it is raining, they will get into something or under something and stay there snug and warm till the rain stops, but this does not mean they are enjoying life any the less because of the temporary enforced inaction. Basically, they enjoy watching the rain happen, even if they do not necessarily want to be wandering up and down in it. The same goes for the snow and the cold. When it is too chilly for the average cat to fancy being out and about, then what can be better than getting curled up into a nice warm corner for a long, safe, soothing snooze? Even sleep is a great pleasure for cats, and if the harshness of the weather gives them the excuse for a longer nap than usual, they are only too happy to take advantage of such an excuse and indulge themselves. Cats just enjoy life, whatever conditions it happens to be offering at any given time or season.

But I sometimes feel that, for the majority of cats (though not for all, of course), the 'summer season when soft is the sun' is the part of the year they like best. Perhaps because the days are longer, perhaps because the sounds are different (there is nothing, but nothing, to beat the authentic sounds of a long slow summer evening in the country, and, to be honest, it is often not bad in city parks either) or perhaps because the weather is a bit more predictable and stable than in the other periods of the year, it seems that many cats get more fun out of living in summer than at other times. I know that, generally speaking, my own cats stay out longer, often far longer, in the summer than in the other seasons. Some of them apparently go off on small trips, because they disappear for days on end, sometimes up to a fortnight, sometimes, indeed, even more. So maybe they've been to the seaside or the Lake District or maybe the Tyrol or Vienna, Budapest or maybe even Bokhara or

Samarkand. Cape North? Moscow? Who can say with cats? They shouldn't have any difficulties with the Channel (creeping on to the ferries, that sort of thing, the way they used to have to) because now there's the Tunnel and any healthy cat worth his salt can do that in no time. One thing is sure: you won't get anything out of them; wherever they've been, that's their business, their secret, and they're just not telling.

Of course, most cats are a bit less daring and adventurous. The least enterprising, timid little things who spend most of their lives looking at you, and checking you out, and seeming to be wondering all the time if they're doing (or if they've done) something wrong, and waiting to be patted and reassured that everything's all hunky-dory, will perhaps creep off timidly for up to three or four hours and then come creeping back apologetically, and you'd swear that what they're thinking is, 'Oh dear, I hope he didn't notice I've been away. I do hope I won't get a scolding,' when you've never scolded the little beggars in their lives precisely because of that timid and delicate air of theirs. However, it is clear that they really do enjoy their summer and yield to all its temptations, in spite of all their mind-forged manacles and repressions. Indeed, it is true that the timidest, meekest, mildest she-cats, that look as though butter wouldn't melt in their mouths and blush to hear of pleasure's name, are the ones that get themselves most outrageously and shamelessly pregnant in the summertime. It must be something in the air.

Then there are the more vivacious cats. Not the ones described above, who have already booked their holidays six months previously and disappear for a fortnight as soon as the summer shows its face, but what we like, slanderously perhaps, to call our dirty-weekenders. They are the ones who vanish for two or three days and then come back a good bit thinner and a bit tanned and all smirking and grinning and giggling, and then they wolf something down and drink lots of water and go to sleep for two or three days before popping out for another session of the same, and you know that whatever they've been doing they've been doing lots of it and they've really been enjoying it and they'll spend the rest of the summer doing it over and over again and then they'll probably join the semi-comatose brigade, if not the deep hibernators, in the winter.

Then there are the real fanatics of the summer. These you recognise only if you are fortunate enough, as I am, to have a nice big garden with centuries-old trees and shrubs and things in it, and members of the family and so on who are crazy enough about plants and stuff to look after it as it should be looked after. In the springtime, my garden is a riot of blossom, but it is in the summer that it really spreads itself and shows at its wonderful, extravagant, flowery best. It is not a huge garden, as gardens go, but it is certainly more than big enough for us to handle on our own, so we have the regular additional help of a growling, grumbling old curmudgeon of a 'gardener' who comes in and, at enormous exorbitant cost (and I hope he is cringing with shame and mortification as he is reading this) turns the whole place, with his wonderful green fingers, into an unparalleled, authentic Garden of Eden (yes, I admit it, Nicholas, *even if it sticks in my throat*).

An authentic Garden of Eden. For us, and for the cats. Nicholas, being a natural grumbler, displays considerable hostility (verbally at least) towards most of the cats, deeming them to be little better than pests on a par with aphids (whatever they may be – gardening is not my field) and moles and Dutch Elm Disease and caterpillars and things like that. Most of them but, curiously, not all. Unbelievable but true, he has soft spots. Not towards the rest of the human race, perhaps, concerning which he is particularly censorious and self-righteous. But Nicholas recognises that some cats are genuine garden-lovers, who particularly enjoy and esteem a nice garden in the warm summer weather. And it is my secret but firm belief that one of the reasons that he brings our humble acre or so to such Babylonian levels of horticultural perfection is precisely because he respects and appreciates those kindred spirits, the garden-lovers in our feline flock. He judges them, no doubt, in his grousing misanthropy, to be closer to himself in essence than all the wretched bipeds with whom he is obliged grudgingly to rub shoulders and share the planet, myself and family included (though I have to admit that, in his miserable way, he is all right with the wife). Well, who cares? Where genius is concerned, it is a good idea simply to turn a blind eye and put up with eccentricities. Better a sullen, bad-tempered gardener of genius than a friendly and affectionate but mediocre one – that is, of course, when you need a gardener *qua* gardener and not as, say, a drinking companion up the pub. And, as several of my cats would agree, and as all my admiring and envious neighbours do agree, and, no doubt as Nicholas himself agrees, not being afflicted with such a banal human weakness as modesty, Nicholas is a genius with bells on, and something to write home about.

A very great gardener is like a very great chef or perhaps a very great conductor of a first-class orchestra. He has his tics and his tricks, his loves and his hates, his moments of temperamental rage, his Dark Days, his frowning, introspective, incomprehensible silences, his moods and his huffs and his airs and his graces and his secrets. He alone knows the right way to mix and blend certain colours and tonalities, certain perfumes, certain nuances, certain subtle shades of the same colours that create such soothing and suggestive effects. He has a sense of time, and an innate insight into light and shade and the effects of dew and of breezes, and, in the heart of the winter, he can already envisage what sort of shadows and scents will be cast by what particular plants and flowers in this very snow-covered spot on a drowsy far-off summer afternoon. If he closes his eyes, he can see it. He understands the aesthetic effects of soil and sand, rock and stone, wood and brick, rain and wind. It is a gift. It is something beyond imagination. It is something beyond instinct. It is something close to what the poets talk about when they're trying to explain what inspiration is. Well, much as it galls me to admit it, Nicholas is all this, and incalculably more, greater, as they say, than the sum of all his parts. Nicholas, as a gardener, is inspired, and the cats know it.

Some cats love lazing about the lawn. Well, we have a lawn, a poor thing but our own. I'm the one who does most of the mowing and the rolling, but the others do chip in with these activities from time to time and they lend a hand with the weeding and getting rid of the odd dandelion or bit of clover or dry tuft. Then the cats come flocking out and flop on it during the warm summer months and roll about on it and try to catch butterflies and dragonflies and things like that on it and have a grand old time to themselves *but I wish they wouldn't claw at the grass like that they don't know how I suffer.*

Many cats enjoy following us in our gardening activities, confirming the old belief that there is nothing quite like watching others work while you yourself are lying lazily on the grass or in a deck-chair or in the cool shade of a tinkling ornamental fountain, exonerated by the nature of your species from any actual fatigue. The expression on a cat's face while he is watching you weeding and destroying greenfly under a hot July sun, in the sure and depressing knowledge that both pests will soon turn up again grinning and sniggering at you behind your back, can be an extraordinarily provoking thing, and on more than one occasion I have taken advantage of the proximity of the hose to wipe that self-sufficient smirk off certain particularly exasperating feline faces. I mean, if they showed willingness to help it would be different, but all that lying around and doing nothing while you are doing something that is getting you hot and sweaty and irascible and you know it's futile anyway . . . No, that's too much to ask of anyone's patience.

Some cats ignore the pleasures of lazing around on the lawn for the more varied pleasures involved in the climbing-up of trees – some by the incredible feat of digging their claws into the bark and literally running up the sides, others by climbing in a more orthodox manner – and, be it said, occasionally the falling-out of them. Some find at a certain point that they have gone too far up and panic and spend the next hour or so screaming their heads off and frightening the neighbours and passers-by and getting the cops and the fire brigade called and then, just when you have arrived running with your brother-in-law-up-the-road's long ladder balanced on your shoulder and practically crushing you to death (and you have never known such pain) they realise the situation is not so dire after all and slip back down with a leisurely, tranquil air and stroll across the lawn to the cat-flap and a spot of milk.

Some cats do not have a head for heights, and nor do they see much fun in lolling around on the lawn all day doing nothing. These take a particular delight in crawling through bushes and shrubbery, or enjoy digging up the stones – for no apparent reason – in the rockery or prowling around damaging the plants in the greenhouse. Such cats have a gangsterish, vandal-istic, juvenile-delinquent spirit which finds its most satisfactory outlet in messing about with plants. Curiously, these cats are of two distinct types, and although occasionally some cats have both tastes, the rule seems to be that some types prefer wrecking decorative plants – particularly delphiniums, lavender, rhododendrons, lilies-of-the-valley and, when they have been recently manured, helianthus and some types of roses, while others, perhaps of more, let us say, *rustic* tastes, prefer to wreak their havoc on the kitchen garden, with a particular inexplicable malice shown towards the humble carrot, the innocuous lettuce, the blushing, retiring radish and the even humbler bean.

And then there are certain other cats who haunt the garden not because they enjoy wandering in and out among the bushes or dozing on the lawn or simply enjoying the flowers and the sunshine and the busy hum of the insects and the growling of Nicholas or having a bit of a wrecking spree or, indeed, eating bits of plant (a surprising number do that, actually, often with unlovely consequences on the grass that we, which usually means *I*, have to clean up). These cats are in the garden because there are birds in the garden and they are after them. Blackbirds, thrushes, sparrows, pigeons. For these cats, summer is not a season, it is a rite, the primitive rite of the hunter, and they are following the oldest instinct of all, the instinct that was millions of years old before *felix catus* and *homo sapiens* first bumped into each other on a hot August night by a lakeside hundreds of thousands of years ago and both thought Now What On Earth Are You? For them, a garden is specially designed as a place to which birds are attracted for the sole purpose that they can grab them and gobble them up. And the summer is the best time for this, because there are more birds around and the weather is generally at its best and because, being hot, the birds are perhaps a little slower and less smart than usual, and consequently a little easier to get at. In these cats, behind the charming veneer of Nicholas's little Eden, beneath the veil of order and civilisation, dark passions reign, the Law of the Jungle obtains, and the Queen's Writ no longer runs through all the long days and slow sunsets and brilliantly starlit nights of summer.

15
Dusty, Rags and Scraps

This is another story (a cat story, or a sort of cat story, when I get there, but I'm taking it easy) that reaches back, as it were, into the mists of time, to a time when I wore shorts and sandshoes and dreadful zigzag patterned jumpers (which zigged and zagged beyond belief) knitted by my grandmother, with the sleeves too long and holes that surely were not part of the Original Plan and the rude and rough boys of the neighbourhood used to yell out WhoWearsShortShorts and worse (much worse, infinitely worse) and beat me up when I was not bright enough to run away from them as soon as I saw them coming which was not at all nice of them but oh well it's all water under the bridge no point in dwelling too much on things like that.

It's a story about an old man who lived in the woods, and if that sounds like one of those daft little stories straight out of folklore I'm so sorry but it isn't I wouldn't dream of writing about any such thing I do have my weaker points but this is not one of them.

This old man who lived in the woods was very, very old when I first actually spoke to him, though I had often seen him around and had known about him from my infancy. I just happened (as was not infrequently the case) to be running away from some of the above-mentioned rough, rude boys of the neighbourhood who were racing after me in the hope of catching me and sacrificing me to whatever dreadful, bloodthirsty minor deity they believed in, and, with them baying at my heels and uttering the most dreadful swear words and the most graphic descriptions of what they were going to do to me when they got their hands on me which left them rather hoarse and breathless, I reached the very edge of our town, just where the woods began.

Those woods belonged to a family who had been there for centuries: I think they had been fortunate enough to get hold of an old abbey at the time of the Dissolution of the Monasteries, and had hung on in there ever since. Not them in person, of course, though some of them looked it, to be quite honest, but as a family. Anyway, I know they gave themselves no end of airs and graces. They were terrible snobs and tended to get people's backs up and they antagonised a great many of their neighbours with their air of superiority and their scorn and dislike of most other people around them. I have known even the mildest-natured people turn pale when their name was mentioned and practically start smoking at the ears.

By the way, I wouldn't really be saying this if it wasn't necessary for this story – as long as people don't bother me I am, like the cats, perfectly happy not to bother them. The fact is that the old man this story is about was himself a member of this ancient family. It seems that, in the final years of Queen Victoria's reign (because, as I say, we're going back quite a while here), he, a local farm labourer's son and by then a handsome young soldier, had come home from the wars covered in glory and medals but with a slight limp and poor as a church mouse and, somehow or other, had met the heiress of this property. She, no doubt bored stiff by all the eligible if chinless young blades busy a-courting her, had promptly fallen in love with this battle-scarred young Adonis from another class and another world. By all accounts she was a very lovely young thing and he, young Robin, had happily returned the compliment by falling equally in love with her.

Naturally, any possibility of their beginning a courtship was quite out of the question. In those days, uppity young rustics could still get quietly and discreetly horse-whipped by their betters out there in the sticks when it was felt they needed teaching a lesson, and in stepping out of line in this way Robin was not asking for a mere lesson but a full-immersion course. But they had fallen pretty heavily for each other, and, well, love has a way of getting round all obstacles: that's what half of world literature's all about, and some of it, as we know, makes really great reading too. The two youngsters decided, like so many other young lovers before and since, that the only remedy was flight, and they duly fled.

They were married somewhere on the Continent. Some say France, some say Spain, some say Switzerland, others Germany, but the fact is that they did run away, and they did get married, in the best romantic tradition, and her family, of course, hit the roof. The idea of one's only daughter and heir getting herself spliced to a penniless, illiterate, landless peasant has never gone down well with the rich (or with the poor, if the truth were told, although often they have less choice in the matter, and anyway they don't usually go on about it quite as much), and in this particularly snobbish family it went down very badly indeed.

They disinherited her, leaving the property to the first heir male of her body or some such legalistic stuff, and although both parents lived for another quarter of a century or more, they refused ever to see her again, cutting her out of their lives for good and all. When their grandchildren, a boy and a girl, were born, they refused to see them either, but they did, through their lawyers naturally, grudgingly put up the money for their education at expensive schools without so much as setting eyes on them even once. They eventually died, by all accounts an old, lonely, sad and bitter couple, within weeks of each other just after the end of the First World War (I think someone told me it was in the great influenza epidemic but I wouldn't swear to that), having modified the will a bit so that the girl would get something too. In the meantime, their unhappy daughter had herself died, never, it seems, having regretted for one moment her choice, and leaving her unhappy ex-soldier, Robin, with only the two kids and the memory of a great and simple love that, if not materially, had given them so much in so many ways. At least, that's what the village said, and that's how I hope, and believe, it went. Robin was then working as a baker's assistant, which, being a floury profession, earned him the nickname of Dusty, by which I knew him, and saved as much as he could from his by no means generous wages in order to give his two children everything he could when they came to him for the holidays.

When the two young people came into their inheritance they moved back to our village. The young man went to Oxford to finish his education and became a lawyer, I think, though he never practised: he had plenty of money and had no need to work for his living. The girl, who was, I believe, nearly as pretty as her mother had been and had inherited a tidy sum from her grandparents, stayed on the property for a couple of years, after which she was snapped up by a chinless wonder with a handle to his name and went off to be Lady So-and-So somewhere in the Midlands. At any rate, she leaves the story at this point.

Or almost, because there is one particular that is to be pointed out here before we leave her. One thing is perfectly clear. Whatever their good points may have been – and they may well have had plenty of them, I am not saying they hadn't – those two youngsters had certainly not inherited their mother's demonstrated indifference to class barriers and things like that. They were more, as it were, throwbacks to their grandparents' type.

Their father – Dusty, as I shall now call him – came with them when they returned to our village, but he did not live in the house with them. Either because he didn't want to or – the village as a whole was convinced – because they didn't want an old peasant, father or no father, living with them in their palatial residence and dropping his aitches all over the place and mucking up their drawing-room and letting them down in front of all their classy chums. Dusty ended up living in a sort of shack at the edge of a lake in the middle of the huge woods forming part of their estate. I know this sounds made up but it's true, cross my heart. They made sure, of course, that he had enough cash for his booze and baccy and his grub and his hobbies, and all he had to do was keep well out of sight, especially when their socialite friends were around, and do his best to help them, and everyone else, forget that he, an honourable and decorated Old Soldier of the Widow of Windsor and rude son of the soil, was their loving parent and father.

And so Dusty lived in his shack in the middle of the woods until it literally fell apart after a heavy storm and flooding, and then his son replaced it with a rather nice, spacious, old-fashioned wooden bungalow with electric lighting and a stove and he had running water and a sort of shower-thing installed nearby. When I first saw him I was a very small child and he was an old, old man with bow legs and a bent back and a limp and a very wrinkled face and a nasty, grim, angry expression, who walked crouched over a very short knobbly sort of walking stick and had big, knobbly, sunburnt, freckled old hands and scared me out of my young wits because I really thought he was some kind of gnome or goblin. Well, I mean to say: living deep in the woods and looking like that! This was no bright-eyed shining young red-coated long-striding hero of long-forgotten colonial wars who had stolen the heart of the young passionate blue-blooded beauty of the land as the Young Men From Nowhere used to do in myths and fairy tales. No, just a tired, toothless and grumpy old man, forgotten by almost everyone, snubbed by time and overlooked by history, maybe with the memory of a great love still warm in, and warming, his breast, occasionally compassion-ately scolded by the owner of the local general store when he was caught out filching small nothings – things too insignificant to be considered shoplifting but still, of course, highly irritating to a small shopkeeper who had to keep an eye on the pennies to be sure of his profits. That was old Dusty: the last of his line, too, because his children had made damn sure they assumed their mother's maiden name, rejecting their own perfectly respectable, if rustic and undistinguished, surname as soon as they came of age.

Anyway, to get back to that morning. With the brutal young louts yelling and shrieking at my heels, I climbed the old wooden fence that cut the wood off from the road, and from the rest of the world, and, more terrified by what lay behind me than by what lay before me, I entered it for the very first time. I had always been an ardent, if precocious, reader of fairy tales, and, consequently the very idea of unfrequented woods was, for me, an idea redolent of mystery and dread. I was, if I remember rightly, really very young.

Those woods were lovely, dark and deep, I seem to recall. I do not remember now if the boys actually followed me in, but I rather think that they did not. Pondering upon it now as I write, I wonder if maybe they were as scared of the place as I was.

After a while, I stopped running and started thinking about where I had ended up. I was scared: I was scared of those boys, and I was also scared of this strange, unfamiliar place, but it dawned upon me that I was feeling yet another sensation. I was curious, curious just like any other small animal that finds itself alone for the first time in a strange forest.

My curiosity was short-lived, being almost immediately replaced by another, equally novel experience. As I was standing panting under a tree, my temples pulsating, my calves aching, and squinting round in the half-darkness, my eyes full of perspiration, to get my bearings and let my heartbeat slow down, I was suddenly extremely shocked and surprised at a feeling of acute, piercing pain in what, for the sake of accuracy, I shall call my left buttock.

I believe I had never felt anything remotely approaching such pain before in my short life, and I believe I have rarely felt such pain ever since. It was simply unbelievable, and I therefore felt myself authorised to let out a horrible, shrill and piercing shriek that startled the whole wood into life, with pigeons thundering up from their nests, rabbits and other small creatures shooting around everywhere with their eyes gaping with imbecile panic, pheasants flapping around like idiots and yelling their heads off, and every imaginable other sort of animal and bird rocketing and tooting and trilling and screeching and going on as if the dreadful thing, whatever it was, had happened to one of *their* buttocks, and not to one of mine.

While I was in mid-scream, I was surprised once more by the repetition of the self-same sensation, this

120

time in my right buttock, and it flashed through my mind that I was fortunate in having only two of them otherwise this dreadful thing, whatever it was, might go on, like the poet's brook, for ever. Dancing and writhing in a rather undignified manner, I whirled round, still shrieking and profaning the stillness of the woods, and found, clinging to that very same buttock, a small, vicious, tattered, hairy thing that really looked like nothing on earth or in the heavens but was evidently of the canine species. As my gyrations slowed down I was able to verify that it was, in fact, an evil little black dog that was not a bulldog but clearly believed it was one, because it was clinging to my bottom like grim death and digging in for however long it took.

Howling and hollering I tried to slap it off, but it was having none of that. Clearly, in its mind it was some kind of great primeval predator that had every intention of dragging me back to its reeking cavern to eat me. It was not big, but it felt big and it clearly believed to its own satisfaction that it *was* big, and I have often felt since that maybe that is more important in a world where genuine self-confidence is a quality worth more than gold. In spite of the tenacity of its grasp, it was also growling, and growling deeply and with purpose, and I seriously began to fear that

I would lose my life – perhaps not a particularly important life but, after all, the only one, not being a cat, that I had.

At that point Dusty appeared on the scene, a cigarette clamped between his lips, his walking-stick in one ancient weathered hand, a slim branch in the other. With a rough 'Gerroff, you!' he gave the little dog a rapid, decisive cut with the supple branch, which effectively induced it to change its mind with reference to its intentions concerning my young and tender existence. It raced, whining theatrically – overdoing it, I felt – for a little clump of shrub, from the heart of which it began barking like a mad thing, clearly intending to remind me that it hadn't finished with me yet, not by any means, and as soon as Dusty was gone it would *get* me.

I turned to thank my rescuer but soon changed my mind. Having driven off the dog, he was now wagging the switch in my direction, and he was also waving his walking stick, which looked far more menacing and dangerous. I began to remember the old saying about the frying-pan and the fire, feeling that I had just made the celebrated leap.

Dusty looked exactly like a malevolent gnome or poison dwarf. His face was all twisted up with malice and potential violence. It is true that he was very old, but it is also true that I was very small, and I began to feel that maybe I would have been better off getting caught by the toughs than ending up in the toils of this old madman and his little savage canine sidekick in the lonely heart of a deep and unfrequented wood.

'What you a-doin' here?' he snapped through his cigarette, speaking an archaic variant of the local rustic dialect, already almost incomprehensible to me in its more contemporary form as usually spoken by the local toughs when they were busy beating me up. 'You-a-come-here-t-le-m-ban-ns-ou-agin? Ileshoyaryalil*bugger*!'

I grasped the last word, but only because it was in italics and underlined. It was not a word that I actually understood, or used myself at that stage in my existence, but somehow I sensed that it was not expressive of goodwill and that it boded no good to me. In this sensation, of course, I was not far from the mark. I was young, but I was not stupid.

'Pardon?' I said politely. My parents had told me not to say pardon, but I said it anyway, instinctively feeling that it was the right word in that context.

'You-come-here-to-let-my-bants-out-agin?' Dusty roared, wagging his stick in a manner that I judged was not at all friendly. 'I'll show you!'

I did not know exactly what it was that he wanted

to show me, but I had no particular desire to see it; I could imagine that pain would be involved. I began to miss the little dog: in comparison with this incoherent old nutcase, he was friendship and goodwill itself – maybe just a bit exuberant.

'No!' I said, stepping backwards and holding up my hands before my face as if to ward off a blow – a blow I was fully expecting. 'It wasn't me, honest.' I had genuinely no idea as to what it was I was being accused of, but I was pretty sure I hadn't done it. After all, this was the first time in my life that I had been in this wood, and I had only come here under the most severe duress anyway.

Dusty was not convinced. He moved towards me, muttering under his breath, his stick trembling in his hand. I continued going backwards, step by step, to keep out of his reach, and he followed me, step for step. The ending was, of course, inevitable. I was, after all, in the middle of a wood. I fetched up with my back against a tree, and he closed in on me. I could see just one or two old yellow teeth in the black hole of his old almost-toothless mouth, and spittle on his old chapped lips, and those horrible old claw-like hands, and I was so terrified I felt a terrible burning in my chest and throat and I wanted to be sick and I just knew I was going to die. I had no alternative. I covered my eyes with my arms to shut out the sight of him and I crouched down with my back jammed against the tree and my knees rammed against my chin and I sent up this horrific yell of sheer terror that went echoing through the woods, and it was ten times louder and stronger than the feeble screeches I had let out when that dog of his was biting my bum. I went on and on until my throat was bone dry and the tears were practically spurting out of my eyes. It certainly had its effect on Dusty. I think, old and senile as he was, it suddenly dawned on him that I was really very tiny, just a small, helpless, terrified child in the middle of a strange wood who had just been viciously savaged by his dog and was now so terrified that all he could do was squat down there, squashing himself against a tree, bawling his heart out.

'Hey hey!' he said, holding out his hand towards me and moving his fingers rapidly as if I was a cat or a dog that needed reassuring. 'Don't you take on like that now. You come along with me, young feller me lad.' He sounded quite concerned, and now he was speaking more slowly I was able to make out what he was saying in spite of the thickness of his accent.

I judged that his change of tone was genuine and I also judged that it was better to obey rather than risk getting him worked up and angry again, so I held out my hand and he took it and he led me through the wood until we arrived at his modest bungalow.

Next to the bungalow there was a large cage and, remembering my readings of Hansel and Gretel, my feelings of panic began to surface once more. Dusty gestured towards the cage and said, 'Them's my bant'ns. You in't lit em out, iv yer?' I looked closely at the cage. Inside were a number of peculiarly small hens, and I suddenly realised what the old man was talking about. I remembered having heard that Dusty's hobby was the breeding of bantams, a special sort of chicken which he exhibited at shows; he regularly won prizes with them. I understood now what he was saying, which, translated, was 'Those are my bantams. You haven't let them out, have you?' and the mystery was solved. Clearly some of the mischievous boys of the neighbourhood had been in the habit of creeping into the wood, opening the cage and letting Dusty's prize bantams out as a prank. I, being a boy and having been found trespassing in the wood, was, logically for Dusty and despite my diminutive size, a prime suspect of the crime. Hence his unthinking rage when he found me.

'No,' I said, 'I've never even been here before.'

'Then 'ow come yer 'ere now?'

I explained that I had been fleeing for my life and went into detail, describing my pursuers and tormentors in highly irate and indignant tones. When I had finished he was chuckling hoarsely and half-crouching down and slapping his calves and thighs, which was probably the late-Victorian manner of expressing amusement in our rural communities. As he laughed the small black dog came slinking out of the trees and crept up to him, no doubt judging that if he was laughing, instead of jumping up and down red-faced and yelling his head off like a mad thing, then it was probably safe to come back home.

When he had finished laughing he went into his bungalow and soon came out again with a big blue and rather shabby plastic mug half-full of an orange liquid.

'You get that down you,' he said (and I am again, to avoid complicating things, translating for you). 'I know boys like orange juice.'

I don't know about boys in general but this boy in particular certainly did, and I needed no second telling but gulped it down. It was delicious and marvellously cool, so I imagine Dusty's somewhat reduced, not to say Spartan, quarters ran to a fridge.

'You liked that, didn't you, you really liked that,' said Dusty, eyeing me admiringly as if I had performed an unusual and splendid feat. I nodded and smacked my lips. Dusty took the mug from me and sprinted – I am sure this is not the right word, all things considered, but at any rate he gave the impression of sprinting – back into his bungalow, returning rapidly with the mug half-full again and a large wedge of cake with icing and a glazed cherry on top.

And he was followed this time, not by the black dog who, after sniffing me as if nothing untoward had ever taken place between us, had wandered off again, but by a cat.

He handed me the mug and the cake with his old brown trembling hands, asking, with a sharp and wily air as if he were already pretty sure of the answer, given my age and species, 'Like cake too?'

I confirmed that I did, indeed, like cake too, and proceeded to prove it irrefutably in the time-honoured manner. The old man stood watching me, puffing on a hand-rolled cigarette and cackling with pleasure, and so it was that the two of us, though the better part of a century stood between us, became friends, and I will say, looking back on it down the arches of the years, good friends.

As I swigged the orange, more slowly this time, and munched the cake, I took stock of the cat rubbing itself against Dusty's leg, and I just couldn't help it, I burst out laughing uproariously because it was the funniest cat I had ever seen. All right, I hadn't seen all that many cats at that stage in my existence, but I had seen some and this was the funniest so far. And if my memory is not playing me tricks, it is still the funniest cat I have ever seen, though I have certainly seen some hilarious cats in my time.

In the first place, though an adult – and I don't know how I knew this, perhaps just through intuition – it was diminutive. I mean *tiny*. I formed the impression that it must have been a bantam cat and, being a bantam cat, it naturally would be tiny, just as Dusty's bantam hens were tiny. I have since learnt that there is no such thing as a bantam cat, and I think it is rather a pity that Dusty did not breed some from his as he did from his chickens, because maybe he would have made a fortune and ended his life rich and famous and might even have got a sort of cat named after him, *Felix Catus Robini* or something along these lines (an honour I wouldn't mind myself, actually).

As well as being tiny this cat had a disproportionately large head, a long neck and a small body, and its forelegs had a peculiar characteristic – the fur grew funny. I mean it looked as though it had had its forelegs trimmed like a poodle, with long fur on the upper and lower parts, and in all the middle part the fur was short. It also had a particularly suspicious and rather pathetic squinty-eyed way of looking at you, with its nose twitching delicately and its whiskers vibrating rapidly, that made me laugh so much I actually fell down and my ribs hurt. Even as I write this now, I am laughing out loud about a poor old cat that has been dead and gone for decades. Its fur was rather scruffy tabby but with a white muzzle and bib, and all four of its paws were white.

And the most striking thing about this cat – the comic aspects apart – was the incredible affection it showed for old Dusty, and the incredible affection that old Dusty showed to it in return. When I first saw it, it was tripping along after him out of the bungalow as he brought me my cake and orange, and for the rest of my stay with him it remained glued to him, actually sitting on his shoe and going to sleep there. No one would have suspected that such a grumpy, forbidding old so-and-so could have had such a soft heart, but you could see he just doted on that cat.

Well, for the next couple of years I went quite often to visit old Dusty. My parents knew about it. At first they were a bit diffident, but they came round with me a couple of times and chatted to him, and once they decided that there was no harm in the old man they let me go and see him whenever I wanted. I actually got quite friendly with the nasty little dog, whose name was Rags, and the little cat, whose name was Scraps, and we often spent a long lazy afternoon together, Dusty supplying the drinks and cakes and conversation and the animals and me supplying – oh, I suppose company, though I did sometimes also help to clean out the bantams' cage. Sometime in the course of those two years the little dog disappeared – I think it got run over because it was always racing out on to the road like a mad thing and barking at cars, and maybe it did it just once too often, though Dusty never actually told me what had happened to it – and so he was left with Scraps the cat. I can still picture him lounging in an old faded deck-chair, with his cloth cap down over his eyes and the inevitable cigarette between his lips, his preposterous cat purring away on his lap, and I still feel touched and grateful when I remember how much he enjoyed my company. I don't know what he got out of it, to be honest, and he never said, but I know he did enjoy it. His face used to light up when I turned up and he always had something in his little larder for me to eat and drink. Who knows, maybe he was just lonely and liked company. Maybe I was something like childhood for him. Or memory. Or maybe I was able to give him something he had never got from his own children.

One night, Dusty fell asleep in his bungalow with a lit cigarette in his hand. His blankets caught fire and he died, asphyxiated in his sleep. His ridiculous little cat, Scraps, had been sleeping, as usual, on his chest, and although it is perfectly clear that he could have escaped – he had his own cat-flap for getting in and out – for some reason he did not. When the firemen got into what was left of the bungalow they found them both there together, suffocated, dead, Scraps on his old master's breast, loyal to the last.

Old Dusty and Scraps the cat and Rags the dog. Oh, that's going back a long while now, a long, long while. Dusty had actually made his will before he died – not that he had all that much to leave, to tell the truth – and he left most of his things to me, including the medals he had won in the old days when he had served under Queen Victoria, and which he had never actually worn, as far as I can tell, in public. I still have them after all these years and writing this story has made me take them out, in their original little old cardboard boxes and century-old tissue paper, and have a good look at them again. There are fourteen of them in all, a pretty impressive number. Six are solid silver, with the Old Queen's effigy on them, and they are rather rare collectors' items these days, especially since they are in absolutely mint state. And one of them is a bronze cross and it has a purple ribbon, not at all faded since that long-ago day he was awarded it, and the words 'For Valour' are written on the cross.

16
Traumas with Tilly

Whiskers was our great historical cat, and we will get to him in due course, but he was not, in fact, quite the first cat that my wife and I took in. We'd passed through ten days of hell with a she-cat called Tilly – we didn't give her that name, she came along with it. And Tilly was a lovely cat, at least to look at, but inside her lurked the soul of a starving viper with sand in its eyes and a vicious migraine because it has spent too much time in the midday sun with a snakebite hangover. And that sort of viper is a viper to avoid, however sorry we may feel for it, take it from me.

I brought her home in a brand new, luxurious cat-carrier – a truly marvellous thing, a sort of limousine or Rolls-Royce for cats. Not that I was the one who bought it. I now firmly believe that her ex-mistress had actually gone out and bought that carrier, in total and reckless indifference to the considerable cost, because she was so delighted at the fact that, finally, she was freeing herself from an authentic, flesh-and-blood nightmare, a dreadful and terrible monster, a creature of the sort that appears only in the most tasteless if not downright nasty tales of folklore, and rarely, to be honest, even there.

Tilly.

Tilly was all calm, cool and collected, of course, there in her little cage throughout the drive home, all perfect cat, purring away peacefully and, in her way, vaguely tunefully, primly and properly washing her paws and cleaning herself up, as if properly preparing for her entrée into new, and hopefully culturally and morally better, circles. But even then, if I remember rightly, I had the sneaking and disconcerting suspicion that maybe, just maybe, I'd bitten off a wee bit more than I could chew, that here was something much bigger, very much bigger, than I was, or ever could be. There was, well, a funny look, a smouldering, dusky glow, a hint or portent of something in those eyes of hers, that I didn't like. That I don't like now either, looking back, not even one little bit. Even now, and years and years have passed, I still shudder when I think of it, and on my screen the liquid crystal freezes before my very eyes as I write this, and the computer says that maybe it's time for a brief pause for breath.

So, anyway, in I go, with my magnificent new cat in its magnificent new carrier. And there on the doorstep is my wife to welcome me with our baby daughter in her arms, and we must have made a lovely little sort of timeless and touching tableau. The baby was just about a year old and we had come to the opinion that a sweet little pussycat for her would be company, fun, something nice to play with, all that sort of thing. We had both had cats at home ourselves when we were youngsters and we had lovely warm memories of them, how friendly they were, what fun they were, how much they made us laugh, how good they had been with us.

Well, Tilly showed us exactly how nice and friendly and warm and good she was by bursting straight out of the carrier as soon as I had opened it and vanishing under the dresser, with eyes flashing violet lightning and her pleasant, urbane purring transformed into guttural, grumbling undertones of thunder, at the same time hissing and spitting and writhing like a panful of boiling oil when you have just thrown in a handful of wet chips. I ask you, is that the sort of thing a decent cat should do when offered a new home? I don't know about me, because I couldn't actually see myself, but the wife paled. The baby daughter paled. The goldfish in its water paled. The turtle I had had for years, normally a phlegmatic enough creature, paled. The sky paled. So I suppose, thinking about it now, that I myself probably also paled, though, as I say, I wouldn't swear to it.

So that's how Tilly introduced herself to her new family. After a while she stopped hissing and spitting, but not because she was relenting or anything like that – I think she had just run out of saliva, and maybe she was scared she might dislocate her jaw or something. A heavy, leaden silence followed, in which my wife and I stared each other in the eyes, deeply perturbed if not yet actually aghast. We were beginning to realise that maybe we'd welcomed under our roof a cat with severe behavioural problems, an attitude problem, problems of temperament and a problem of self-control – altogether very much a *problem* cat. Maybe not her fault, of course, but, well, that didn't make things any easier or the outlook any brighter – or the place any safer.

'Maybe she's just hungry,' my wife faltered. 'Let's try giving her something to eat.'

'What did you have in mind?' I said, unable to resist

my usual idiotic urge to crack silly jokes at the wrong time. 'A human sacrifice?'

A noise rose from under the dresser, oddly similar to the sound of a Formula One car testing its motors in the distance. It was just Tilly, testing her motors under the dresser, whence I could almost feel brimstone and sulphuric vapours rising towards us and vaguely see a faint, pulsating, infernal glow.

'Maybe she's scared,' my wife said. That made me laugh. Lots.

'Good for her,' I said, 'and so am I.'

At that point the baby, no doubt sensing a certain tension in the atmosphere, began to scream.

And from under the dresser a new noise uprose, low, tremulous and muted at first, but not for that any the less disconcerting, any the less sinister, which began to mutate into a grotesque, jabbering parody of song, wordless, profoundly morbid, hair-raising; gradually it rose, rose, rose, in power, volume and tonality, until it became a long, horrid, adagio screech suspended between a yodel and a sustained yell of pure rage.

The baby turned up the volume and the cat turned hers up some more; the baby reciprocated and the cat returned the compliment; the baby began to get properly peeved, filled her lungs and really let rip, and the cat, not to be outdone by a malodorous, hairless, pink, toothless critter without as much as a set of whiskers, followed suit. Neither of them showed the slightest consideration for the feelings of the others present (I mean myself and my wife) but fully and unscrupulously indulged their darkest and profoundest urges and impulses. The duet that followed was horrible. It would have delighted Dante to the very soul and maybe have inspired another *Canto*.

There is no point in digging up the past. There is no point in going over what, how much and how terribly we suffered. It would only grieve the reader and reopen old wounds, both mental and physical, and would resuscitate so many dreadful memories which it took us years of pain and effort to allay. Suffice it to say that, after ten days, I took Tilly, spitting and swearing to the last, back to the bosom of her original family (who, I more than suspect, did not welcome her with open arms). There was not a stick of furniture in our entire house that did not bear witness to her short stay: deep scratches in rather beautiful pieces of antique furniture that were – or, I should say, had been – of a certain value; armchairs and sofas gutted; carpets shredded; plates, glasses and vases smashed to smithereens; claw-marks on the fridge, the washing-machine, the dishwasher, the television screen, even on the toilet-bowl; books torn to pieces; records wantonly vandalised; windows broken. I suddenly understood how Europe had felt as the smoke settled after the fall of the Roman Empire and in the aftermath of the first waves of the barbarian invasions. And, to cap it all, we had to contend with a certain chill, a certain resentful stand-offishness, not to say seething hostility and grumbling threats of legal action and physical violence, in which I regret part- icularly foul epithets were also used, on the part of our next-door neighbours. They cannot really be blamed, when I think about it now, and I take the present opportunity of apologising to them here, after all these years; I hope they are enjoying the weather and everything Down Under. They had been singled out by destiny for something strange and terrible, for the privilege of enjoying Tilly's unusual gift of song, night and morning, twenty-four hours a day, for ten days on end, with particular peaks of excellence around three o'clock in the morning and then long, peculiar, mournful ululations towards dawn. I think it broke their spirits.

It was shortly after that that they emigrated to Australia, silently and stealthily and by night, without even saying goodbye to us. As far as I know they have never been back to the Old Country, but have made for themselves, I hope, a better and happier life, far from us, far from Tilly, in Our Antipodes, enjoying the aubade of the koala and the kookaburra and the kangaroo, and I hope they will break a frothing tube and drink my health as they read this, humming 'Waltzing Matilda' in their rude outback tent, with the corks bobbing round their hats, the dingo snoozing at their feet, the razorback grunting serenely among the eucalyptus and the Southern Cross blazing in the night sky.

Tilly's original owner had cheerfully assured us that she would take her back without any problem if we found she had difficulty in settling in, but now I suspect that there was more than a hint of insincerity in her assurances. Certainly she did take her back, but with very great – indeed, I would say extreme – reluctance, with a grim, dry, unforgiving expression on her face that I would swear most certainly wasn't there when I was taking Tilly away ten days previously. No, indeed: then it had been all smiles and sherry and cucumber sandwiches. But then was then and now was now. Tilly was thinner than she had been: at our house, she had only eaten the things that she shouldn't have eaten, including, for example, several pages of my first edition of George du Maurier's *Trilby*, and I know I never found one of my favourite gloves again and – well, I have my suspicions. We had showered that cat with all the luxuries money could buy, in the pathetic – and fatuously vain – hope of winning her over and converting her to goodness through kindness and, as far as it was within our power, love. She had flung them back in our teeth with vicious sneers and jibes and with contempt and violence, and now here she is, skinny as a rake, and her owner taking advantage of this to place her hands on her hips and rake me with similar derision and contempt and dryly say: 'But look at the state she's in, just skin and bones! What on earth have you been doing to her?'

I willed her to look at me. I willed her to see me with the eyes of charity and understanding. I, too, was just

skin and bones. As were the wife, the baby, the goldfish, the turtle, the neighbours, and, as far as I could see, the rest of the Solar System.

'You don't know what she's been doing to us!' I said, equally dryly, striving, though not very hard, to keep a note of indignation and accusation out of my voice, but my shoulders were bent and my hands trembled and my eyes were red and my voice was a broken, reedy, unmanly whisper. And then I saw a gruesome flash of pure sadism in those eyes of hers and the truth dawned on me in all its horror – she did know, *of course she knew*.

17
Remembering Whiskers (1)

One would have imagined that an experience of the sort we had passed through with Tilly would have caused us to abandon any desire to have a 'Cat about the place'. Indeed, few would have blamed us if we had been caught roaming the highways and byways by night in cloaks and masks, looking for cats to take out – and I do not mean take out to dinner, I mean take out. But anyone who has grown up with cats around knows perfectly well that it would take a heck of a lot more than that to discourage the real cat-lover. Time passed. Our wounds healed. With therapy, the wife got better and the baby recovered her composure. We got the furniture mended, or threw it out and bought more, madly indifferent to mounting debts. The nightmares became less frequent. All of us, me, wife, baby, goldfish, turtle, neighbours, postman and so on, began to recover our appetites, began to recover brightness of eye and firmness of limb and our natural muscle tone and that sort of stuff. It was proof of the resilience of the human spirit (though, to be honest, the goldfish and the turtle were not exactly human, but they did stick with us through thick and thin, and we will not deny them the recognition, indeed the respect and honour, which is their due – thanks Fish, thanks Turtle, 'Gone before but not forgotten and a credit to your race/s').

Tilly became a memory – a nasty memory, it is true, but one that became weaker and weaker with time because of our genuine determination to get the whole thing behind us as quickly as we could and recover our mental equilibrium and start Believing In Life again. Then came one wonderful bright sunny morning (to be honest, it may have been a dreary, drizzly, foggy afternoon, or the rain might have even been pouring down in buckets; I cannot really swear as to the weather – it is such a changeable thing hereabouts – after all this time but I hope the reader, who is by now, I dare to hope, a friend, will not mind this overmuch because it is surely the thought that counts) when we found that we could say the word 'cat' again, out loud, without starting to gibber and checking our blood pressure, and we realised that the final road to recovery now lay before us and that Time, the great healer, and Oblivion, his sidekick, were – well, doing what they are paid to do, which is *healing*.

A friend of ours who lives right out in the country rang us up one day and in the course of a conversation with my wife told us about a neighbour of hers whose cat had just had six kittens. Now, when I hear the word 'neighbour' I always get itchy and feel a bit diffident and wish I had a gun or, if I have been drinking, a chain-saw to reach for, but since these were not my neighbours but someone else's, I decided to give them the benefit of the doubt.

Anyway, she said that these kittens were real little stunners. And she, by the way, was highly qualified to judge in these matters, indeed more qualified than we were, because she was absolutely mad about cats. The last time I saw her, by the way, she was living up in the Highlands in an old farm she had bought for a song and – and I'm not exaggerating – she had no fewer than twenty-six cats and eight 'beautiful kittens for deserving family with garden' all lined up like ducks. Naturally, we took one of them, to add to our herd, but that's another story.

She told us of these six kittens, describing them in scrupulous and minute detail, singing their praises in that rather crazy but quite endearing and deeply persuasive manner that only the true cat-lover can achieve. I, for some peculiar reason that even now I cannot quite explain, was struck by her description of one of them in particular: 'Oh, he's a tiny little fellow, black and white, a real Sylvester, absolutely full of beans. You should just see him jump, see him play, and then he's so friendly . . .'

My curiosity was aroused. I have always believed that bi-coloured cats are the best – black and grey, black and ginger, black and white. Especially black and white. I like all normal cats, ordinary common-or-garden cats with no pomposity about them.

Anyway, the wife and I talked things over, and we came to the conclusion that one bad apple – Tilly of unbeloved memory – didn't mean all cats were rotten. We discussed the matter with the goldfish and the turtle, not wishing to spring any nasty surprises on them, and invited them not to judge all cats by Tilly. They were sagacious creatures, and though they said nothing actually in favour of a new cat around the place (we could not really expect that of them) they said nothing against it either, and we therefore took their silence as consent. We reopened diplomatic relations with the postman, whom Tilly had badly traumatised. We told our friend that when the black-and-white kitten was properly weaned we would be willing to take it if no one else put in a prior claim. Then, for the next few weeks, we basically forgot the whole thing.

I think it was about five weeks later that our friend came round for dinner. And along with her came this little black-and-white creature, snuggled down and sleeping peacefully in her chaotic handbag. He was a little beauty – as she had said, a typical Sylvester. His fur was perfect, an exact split between the black and the white, an effect of near-perfect symmetry in his face, his paws, his feet. Needless to say, we rather took to him at once. I'm not sure why but we decided then and there to give him the rather bland and unimaginative name of Whiskers. However, I will state here and now in our defence that, small as he was, it really was one of the first things you noticed about him – a magnificent set of whiskers that would have stung to the quick with envy, to the very soul, Napoleon III or the Kaiser or even Hercule Poirot himself.

Whiskers was not the typical kitten, all fun and games and hyperactivity and leaping up and down everywhere and turning everything and everyone around him into his own personal funfair. He wasn't really one for playing games but, even as a kitten, preferred more restful activities most of the time, interspersed every so often with outbreaks of explosive, volcanic energy. Above all, he was an affectionate cat. He enjoyed playing with lollipops, which he would run and fetch for you time after time after time, like a little dog going after a stick, and he would display profound if impermanent and possibly somewhat insincere grief when the fragile things inevitably got smashed. But for much of the time he just hung around whoever was nearest, purring away and getting himself stroked for a bit, after which he would drift contentedly into sleep. The contrast with Tilly was, of course, immense. Whiskers was a restful cat, and just what we needed to reconcile us with cats as a species – it was almost, indeed, as if Whiskers somehow sensed this, somehow *knew*. Tilly had been more, let us say, of a combination of a natural disaster with a scorched-earth policy united with a *Blitzkrieg* than a normal cat; Whiskers, on the other hand, was of a reposeful nature, philosophical, inward-looking, with more in him of *Il Penseroso* than the *Allegro*, more the Thinking Cat than the Cat of Action.

He was also a creature of habit. Right from the very start he formed the habit of wandering into our bedroom bright and early in the morning and hopping on to the bed for a brief little final snooze before facing the manifold fatigues of the day. As time went on, he improved upon this single, simple ritual by strolling up the eiderdown, settling down on my chest and washing my beard. This gradually became his way, gentle and refined as he was, of courteously and ceremoniously inviting me to start thinking seriously about getting out of bed and maybe fixing him a spot of breakfast. Once he had managed to get me up and out of the bed, he would settle down for another forty winks while I got myself sorted out. Then, when he heard interesting things happening downstairs, he would hop down from the bed and, without haste or anxiety, join me politely in the kitchen, waiting with languid nonchalance for his breakfast. When I see him now, as I gaze back down the long colonnade of the years, I think of the scandalous way the cats of the present generation behave when they are waiting for their breakfasts and lunches and things, and I sigh and bow my head wearily and yearn for the good old days when cats were polite and clean (yes, clean, Clovis, clean) and self-respecting, and ask myself where all the good manners went.

In spite of his normally gentlemanly, urbane behaviour, Whiskers was, to say the least, rather an unpredictable cat. From an early age, he showed an unhappy and distressing tendency in favour of substance-abuse. He enjoyed getting cheaply stoned by sniffing bleach, which I feel is not a thing to be encouraged in cats. Not that he took it neat, of course – that would have been really worrying – but his thing was to hang around waiting until we had wrung out the bits and pieces of laundry we had left in bleach for a bit to get the dirt out, and then he would creep, or rather sneak, over when our backs were turned, and sniff them and roll about in them until found out and driven off, and then he would wander around the house with his pupils dilated and his mouth ajar and a dreamy, idiotic look on his face, walking into the walls and miaowing pleasing little songs to himself, *sotto voce*.

After a bit the effect would wear off and he would simply keel over and drop off to sleep, lying there absolutely motionless for an hour or so, sometimes with one eye, sometimes even with both eyes, half-open. He didn't really care where he was – in the kitchen, in the bathroom, in the garden, more than once up a tree (though God knows how he got up there), on the dining-room table, in the coal-shed. The first time he did it, he really gave me a scare. I was convinced he was dead, but it was only a sort of drunken stupor. When he came out of it, he was normally a bit down for a while – we called it his bummers – and I think it possibly gave him a bit of a headache. We ended up closing him out of the house when the laundry was being done: we didn't want to end up with a feline junkie on our hands.

Whiskers had been with us for just about two years when he died. It was all my fault. It was in the summer. Whiskers came home one day full of fleas. It wasn't a matter of the odd flea that almost every cat carries about with him to have a little light entertainment, a little something to do when he is feeling at a loose end. Whiskers had, to scale, the equivalent of the *Grande Armée*.

So I went out and bought one of those anti-flea collars and, just to be sure, a packet of anti-flea powder. I put the collar on him – he didn't like it one little bit but, being Whiskers, a polite and trusting animal, he accepted the situation calmly, never caring to kick up a fuss. Then I sprinkled some of the powder on his coat, just to be on the safe side. The next day I sprinkled on some more. I didn't read the instructions.

Too much powder got into his system, when he was washing himself, I think, or maybe he just breathed too much into his lungs. He fell ill. He spent a couple

152

of days coughing and sneezing under the sofa and he
wouldn't eat and he wouldn't come out. Then he died.
We were very unhappy. Our friend came round and
helped out and we took him home and buried him on
the farm where she had got him.

We were, of course, totally prostrated for some
time by the death of our sweet cat, and I was
particularly stricken because of my feelings of
personal responsibility and guilt. I knew it was all my
fault and my unhappiness was aggravated by quasi-
moral considerations: I considered that the animals
we welcome into our homes, which in effect we
adopt, depend on us for a great deal – food, shelter,
warmth, security, affection, tranquillity. And in these
things I, however involuntarily, had failed. As a result
of my carelessness and my stupidity, I had caused the
death of a creature that had had every right to expect
from me protection and care and safety, at the very
least. My wife – who did not learn the whole truth for
several months, so ashamed was I of what I had done
– spoke from time to time of getting another cat. She
saw I was very glum and disorientated for quite a
considerable period after the death of our poor
Whiskers and she thought that another cat around
the place would help me to get back on an even keel.
But I refused even to discuss the matter. I had already

done enough damage with one cat, and I did not want to repeat the experience.

But Time and Oblivion rolled up their sleeves and got to work again. I began, gradually, to see the whole business from a slightly different angle. There was no need, just because I had made one stupid mistake, to believe that I would do the same thing again. After all, we learn from our mistakes. And by then my daughter, who was now able to talk, was always going on about wanting another cat – 'just like Whiskers,' she used to say. Our poor Whiskers had worked his innocent and gentle magic on her, too.

18
The religion of cats

There seems to be so much talk about religion today, and a lot of it so irrational and angry that it seems only right and proper to include animals in the debate. After all, if there is a God, and he created us, then he created them, too, and maybe they should have some say in the matter. (It goes without saying that they have souls, by the way.) And the fact is that cats generally show so much good sense about things that maybe their opinions on this subject, too, as in so many other things, could be of some help to us. We should listen to our cats more. More than so many of the people we generally tend to listen to, because – well, see where they go and land us, let's just put it that way.

One thing is sure: if any cats are religious fanatics or fundamentalists or whatever, they are certainly keeping very quiet about it. They don't go running around with scowling faces and odd dress accessories or jewellery or weaponry (for God's sake!) or whatever to show their adherence to this or that religion, or turn up their noses at this or that sort of food or turn up their noses at those who *eat* this or that sort of food or get angry because you belong to this sect of the faith or that sect of the faith or the other sect of the faith and not their sect of the faith and all that sort of thing. Very wise of them.

It is reasonable to suppose that the religion of cats would be something solar, perhaps the quiet and discreet adoration of an ancient figure like Apollo or his predecessors the Egyptian Aton or Shamash, the ancient and wonderful sun deity of the Middle East. Or, thinking about it, given their penchant for sitting on walls at night and yelling at the moon, maybe their preference would be for a feminine lunar divinity like Artemis or the deathless Diana of the Ephesians – or if they prefer a masculine figure there is always Sin, the moon god of old Babylonia, or Nanna, his Sumerian counterpart. Nor should we forget the figure of Bast, the cat divinity of the ancient Egyptians, another feminine lunar deity as a matter of fact. Or it is possible that they pay due and meet adoration to lesser gods, the ones that, their status eroded with time, became our elves and fairies, the immemorial minor deities of the brooks and the rivers and the fountains and waterfalls, the gods of the caverns and the hills and the fields and the meadows, of the valleys and the plains, of single trees and of entire forests, that were so much part of the simple piety of ancient times and of times reaching back far, far beyond recorded history, into arboreal sunrises and sunsets we cannot even begin to imagine, not even in our richest and most beautiful, or most troubled, dreams.

Certainly, cats would have a lot more difficulties with the more complex religions humanity has gone and landed itself with over the last couple of millennia. They would feel very uncomfortable about all the paranoid squabbling that goes on over the specific identity of the Divine Being and the sort of things he considers important: whether you should wear a duffel coat with toggles or with buttons, which of your neighbours are saved and which are damned, what language he speaks, what he likes to have for his dinner and what he wants you to have, and not to have, for your dinner, and what he wants you to do in your spare time and all that sort of thing.

It's interesting, in this context, to remember Hamlet's exchange with Polonius about the cloud:

Polonius: My lord, the Queen would speak with you, and presently.

Hamlet: Do you see yonder cloud that's almost in shape of a camel?

Polonius: By th'mass, and 'tis like a camel indeed.

Hamlet: Methinks it is like a weasel.

Polonius: It is backed like a weasel.

Hamlet: Or like a whale.

Polonius: Very like a whale.

Well, some people see the camel, and some see the weasel, and some see the whale. Others, had they been there, would have seen – who knows? – rabbits or sheep or goats and monkeys, or, like Polonius, they would have seen whatever they had been told to see. And people see their God as they have been told to see him by their Hamlets, and as they, squinting their eyes, see him themselves, or want to see him.

The more balanced and perspicacious, of course, would have resisted the power of suggestion and would have seen the cloud itself, and would have recognised, in spite of the mutations of its form, its essential cloudness, something that transcended all the illusions that people were building up around it.

And the most perspicacious would gently remind us, just to get a dialogue going, that there are plenty of other clouds around, too, and they are not so very different, though some do look a bit like ... well, some do look a bit *funny*.

Cats are pragmatic. Cats are wily, and when they are not waggling them in the air, they have their feet on the ground. Cats would see through all that. Cats wouldn't form theories about what clouds look like; they would not even bother trying to get at the real nature of the cloud; cats have nice big eyes and they can see a long way, and cats, of course, would see the cloud but they would also see around the cloud and behind the cloud and see the sky itself, the element in which these clouds float and exist and have their being. Perhaps, then, their religion would express itself in the humble acknowledgement of some great big principle like Karma or Brahma or Maat of the Egyptians or Confucius's Tian or the Fate of the Classical World or the Wyrd of the Anglo-Saxons – although it is better not to try to pin it down with a name or names because, as every cat knows, the Way which we can call the Way is not the Way. Certainly the cats' religion would not be formed of, or bound by, customary and inherited rules and regulations and beliefs that are the inventions of a particular ethnic group for their particular ethnic group, organised and systematised by no doubt very great and wonderful individuals: inventions that then, unhappily, got out of hand and spread beyond their natural confines and fell into the wrong hands, infecting our long-suffering continents with all the consequences of faiths that were originally intrinsically good but then often botched and contaminated and badly lived, centred on bigotry and xenophobia and rancour and lust for power and fear.

No. I bet that's not the way cats live their spiritual side, not by a long chalk. Sometimes, when I see a cat crouched under a bush, rapt in the observation of raindrops dripping from the leaves of the trees on to the twinkling grass below, gleaning wisdom; or when I see him sprawled along a bough for all the world like a tiny little panther, his nose twitching and his whiskers bristling as he absorbs all the passing sounds and odours, silent messengers of the universe, I begin to feel that maybe Kenneth Grahame hits the nail on the head in *The Wind In the Willows* when he talks about the mysterious and elusive sylvan figure of the Piper at the Gates of Dawn. Just as we re-dimension the ineffability of the Divine Principle into something congenial to our history and culture and sense of identity, like Christ or Krishna or Buddha, so cats could well be doing something similar through a synthesis of the animal and the human. Their figure of godhead could well be a rather whimsical one of a benign and caring Pan-like being, having in him the best of Human and the best of Animal, which he expresses through the mild and gentle and harmonious music of the forest. And this is accompanied in certain passages, I like to think, by the Aeolian Harp, and maybe even, in symphonic moments, by the Music of the Spheres, and the sung Numbers of Pythagoras, bringing peace and tranquillity and a sense of safety and security to small and bewildered creatures living in a world which, when all is said and done, is not very kind to them and is often so very hard for them to understand. Especially Clovis, our dirty cat, and our one-eyed Ronald.

19
Remembering Whiskers (2)

With time, it became clear that, yes, we would eventually have another cat, and it was tacitly understood that it would be another black-and-white cat, like our poor lamented Whiskers. And, naturally, it was quite impossible to find one answering to such a description. That's always the way with cats. When you don't want a cat of a particular type the whole world seems to be heaving with them. If you don't want a black-and-white cat, there seem to be so many of them around that the whole world seems entirely populated by black-and-white cats, with human beings hanging around on the margins like a colourful side-show, an interesting and rare species on a par with unicorns or white elephants or the Abominable Snowman. When you're looking for black-and-white cats, you'll find cats of every possible nuance of the spectrum from pale violet to phosphorescent green with orange stripes, but you won't find a black-and-white cat, not even for ready money. The secret is to pretend you don't want a black-and-white cat, you wouldn't dream of having a black-and-white one: say you want a blue one, or one with ears like a rabbit, or a gay one, or a vegetarian one, and then maybe, just maybe, somebody'll say, 'Well, actually we haven't got anything quite like that at the moment. Pity you didn't come last week . . . We do have a teeny-weeny black-and-white one, though, if you want to have a peek. Quite without obligation, of course.'

Given the dearth of black-and-white cats on the market, we considered adopting this or that kitten, deciding to forget our fixation for one type in particular. Then, one day, my wife came home from the school where she was teaching and told me that one of her pupils had told her that she had several kittens ready for adoption, and that one of them was black and white.

We decided, then and there, to take it. My wife got her pupil's address, and one evening I got on my bike with a little box that had contained a pair of my daughter's shoes and I cycled off to fetch this new little candidate for the feline role in our family circle. After a ride of about three kilometres I arrived at the address I had been given. It was a nice little Victorian detached house – Clare Villa it was called, if I remember rightly – with a nice little lawn in front, and there, beside a little goldfish pond, was a basket. Inside the basket was Mother Cat, a little tabby with only three legs, and there were four or five kits leaping up and down, dancing, punching the air, squeaking, rolling around, stalking and nipping and biting and scolding each other, and Mother occasionally joining in with a slap for this one and an indignant hiss at that one; and in the midst of all this frenzy, this madhouse, there was this little black-and-white chap who paused suddenly to stare at me with big round eyes so full of vitality and *joie-de-vivre* that – yes, you guessed it – he captured my heart immediately. And so it was that I first met Whiskers the Second, Whiskers II, *Whiskers the Great*.

The leave-taking was brief. I chatted a little with the girl's mother, while the girl herself went through the time-honoured ceremonial thing of getting the kitten to say goodbye to its mum and putting a little bright blue ribbon round its neck. Then we put it into the little shoe-box, which I secured with some string and

164

placed carefully in the bike's basket, just the right size for it. Naturally, I had already made the usual but *de rigueur* holes in the box just to make sure the kitten had enough air and light. Then I got on my bike, said goodbye to mother and daughter and Mum and siblings, and rode off into the sunset with our new family member.

It was small, but that little creature packed one hell of a voice. I could hear it scratching away in its box as I pedalled, trying to dig its way out as if it thought it was in Colditz or something. Every so often a tiny spotless white paw or a tiny twitching pink nose would poke out of one of the holes then vanish back inside. Then it would let out the occasional long, shrill, mournful and desperate scream, especially, and seemingly on purpose, when I stopped at the traffic lights, which could be extremely embarrassing. People would stare, first at me then at the box in the basket, with an interrogative and critical air that made me feel all hot and bothered and grin at them apologetically, thinking that they were convinced I was some kind of sadistic monster who got his kicks by cycling round the countryside with cats shut in boxes just to make them scream. I remember one old lady in particular, a nasty-looking piece of work, all nose and Persian lamb and umbrella at the traffic lights, who gave me a very dirty look; she was one of those senior citizens who seem to have a special gift for contorting their features into grotesque masks of the most indescribable, sheer intimidating nastiness, and I'm pretty sure I heard her mumble, 'Now I'm going to get the police on you!' but then the lights changed and I started pedalling harder and harder and got home, hot and red-faced and sticky and sweaty and as if all the hounds of hell were on my traces, but with my little box and its small but vociferous contents intact.

I was a little worried as I carried the screaming box indoors. I remembered Tilly and how she had shot out of that cat-carrier, grim and determined and armed to the teeth, to begin her reign of terror right from the outset. Maybe this kitten was so traumatised by his voyage in a shoe-box that his character was marred for life; maybe he had become a wild beast, and by God would he make us pay for this to the last miserable drop of our blood.

I needn't have worried. Looking back, I think he actually enjoyed that little trip in the box. I undid the string in the presence of my wife and daughter, and out poked this funny, happy little face, just like poor old Whiskers but with a comical little black blot round its nose and a neat little black patch, like a beard, under its chin.

'It's Whiskers! Back!' my daughter cried, delighted.

And so, spontaneously, we decided that he *would* be Whiskers, Whiskers the Second, in memory of our old pal. There was no question of lack of respect or feeling for his predecessor, but really, in a certain sense and though we knew we were kidding ourselves, it was a bit like having him back again. The two cats were so similar, except for those negligible differences, that though this one was still a tiny kitten, it really did seem, in many ways, the same animal. We would never, of course, cease to feel our old affection for our original Whiskers, but in a funny sort of way we could feel it, and in a happier sort of way, through this new one. Well, I know it sounds odd; it's a mystery, but that's how pets work, as most seasoned pet-owners will confirm.

'It's not really Whiskers,' I told my daughter, wishing to be honest with her.

'Well, it's Whiskers Two!' said my daughter, with the bright, careless logic of infancy, clapping her hands. 'Whiskers! Lovely!'

And she was right, of course: it was a lovely little cat.

Whiskers began working his magic right from the start. As soon as he got out of that box, he began dancing around the room on tiptoe, his back arched, blowing curious little raspberries. We just fell about laughing at the sight of him. He was irresistible – an overworked word, perhaps, but there is just no other that works better here. It seems that he really did want to make the right sort of impression on his new family at the very outset, and there is no doubt that he succeeded. He was full of life and energy and joy. He raced around the house, up and down the stairs, all over the furniture, up and down the curtains, trembling with curiosity and really giving us the impression that he could actually fly. The first thing that really struck you about him was that he had an enormous sense of fun – and let's be honest, that's something that probably every cat-lover really wants from his cat more than anything else.

Then, boy, could he eat! Over the years I've come to realise that the first great worry when you get a new animal, of whatever type, in the house is whether it's going to start eating or not, probably because we feel instinctively that if the creature is eating all right it means that it is more or less at ease with its new setting, and, by extension therefore, with its new family. Food involves much more than simply eating. It involves much more complicated impulses and drives. It is enough to remember the ancient traditions among various races and peoples of things like sharing salt, or breaking bread together, or the timeless rituals, practically ethics, related to hospitality itself. Eating together means, temporarily at any rate, sharing the same food habits and the same dietary values and restrictions and taboos, but it also, by extension, means safety, means friendship – and not doing so, sadly, often means quite the opposite, means enmity and fear.

Well, anyway, there was no problem of this sort with our Mr Whiskers. He started tucking in at once, and with immense zest and conviction. He incarnated the concept of a hearty eater, and was not in the least bit fussy about what he ate, either. He was not one of your prissy cats. He had a neat little solid white paunch, which tended to – well, swell when he was eating; it showed that he liked to eat what I shall euphemistically call 'a lot', and it was a genuine joy to watch him at it. I had better add at once, because this is not a negligible element when we receive a new cat in the house, that he immediately learnt where he had to go when he had to do what he had to do – his duty, as the Victorians used to put it – and he began making use of the conveniences placed at his disposal right from the start. Many cat-owners consider this sort of adaptability as a sign of feline intelligence, and we, of course, immediately began to consider Whiskers as a sort of genius of the first water, a pardonable weakness on our part which most people with pets will, I believe, readily understand and forgive.

Whiskers, we realised at once, was clearly a cat of an autonomous and independent nature, but he had a great ability – and, I would say now, *need* – to express affection. And he wanted, or again needed, to receive it, too. He liked to get cuddled and patted and chatted to, and he was the sort of cat that came for a snooze on your lap right from his kittenhood. He would sleep on your knees, or on your bed, or on the sofa snuggled up against you, or in the crook of your elbow in the armchair while you were trying to read (which was not an easy thing to do, especially if it was a news-paper or an atlas), or on your pullover if you left it lying around, or on top of your slipper to make you feel guilty when you tried to get it back or – or anywhere, really, except in his own basket, which was always his last and least favourite choice, and he would only go there when peremptorily sent, and even then grumbling. I believe he didn't like his basket because he didn't like to see himself relegated to the role of a pet, of 'the nice little pusskins in his nice little basket . . . Look at him! Isn't he sweet? . . . Coochy coochy coo.' No thanks. He wanted to participate actively in the family and do the things the family did. I think, to be honest (although this might sound a bit ridiculous or even a bit nutty but, really, lots of animals I have known are like that), he saw himself more as a person than as an animal.

He was a great sleeper. He slept a lot, all his life, having a strong component of laziness, of genuine, inimitable feline laziness, in his make-up. But when he was awake it was a totally different kettle of fish. He was a cat who always had something or other to do – a cat, believe it or not, with hobbies. He had a collection of all sorts of objects which he used to stash away in unreachable places under the furniture, and very often we would find that he had objects of the same type grouped together: so, for example, there was the wardrobe in the hall under which he tended to store, squirrel-like, his small but impressive collection of cheap plastic cigarette lighters. Sometimes, of a rainy afternoon, he would get one or two of them out from under the wardrobe and play around with them, but they always ended up back under there when he had done with them, either by chance (if the reader is cynical) or by design (if, like me, the reader has more imagination, or more credulity, or just more faith in his cats).

When we moved the furniture for some great (and

rare) cleaning operation, or maybe to change the look of the room, we would uncover – to his acute, offended and possessive yells of protest – Whiskers's collections. He had the instincts of the magpie united with those of the kleptomaniac. He was not a normal cat. Glass marbles. Beads. Rubber balls. Elastic bands. Toys from chocolate eggs. Coins. Bones. Objects and furnishings from doll's houses. Brooches and objects of bijouterie. Pencils. Rubbers. Balls of wool. Indescribably chewed and mutilated pieces of plastic. Dried peas and beans. Macaroni. Stones. Matchboxes. Sometimes with discrimination, often with none, he collected or indeed stole (because he often knew he shouldn't be running off with certain things) all sorts of objects, and deliberately hid them where it was difficult for us to get at them. Yes, perhaps if you go back far enough along the tree of evolution, there really was something of the squirrel in that animal. It seems that he sifted every part of the house in order to bring – either in his mouth or kicking them along like a footballer – his ill-gotten gains to the sitting-room, where there was a fair variety of bits and pieces of heavy furniture to choose from and whence, he doubtless reasoned, it would be some time, if ever, before they returned to the light of day. And when we did eventually get round to moving the furniture for one

172

of the occasional reasons described above, he would be lounging around, with an anxious and somewhat suspicious and guilty air about him, knowing that yet another of his illicit troves was about to be unearthed, and uneasily awaiting the inevitable scolding when some outrageously heinous crime should come to light. That look on his face made us laugh even more than the quantity and diversity of the treasures revealed.

He was also a great hunter. Of lizards and insects, that is: it's not that he wandered around the jungles in a pith-helmet and wielding an elephant gun. There are no jungles round our way, nor have there been for several million years. Nor are there elephants, though it must be said that Clovis, our dirty cat, does look a bit like one coming up the garden path when he's been stuffing himself for the winter.

Whiskers really enjoyed one particular sport, in which he could exhibit a rare and enviable skill: he could catch flies in flight. Then he would eat them, which we found a bit disgusting, of course, but he seemed to enjoy them; and who knows, maybe they're full of proteins and low in calories and that sort of stuff and maybe we should try eating them too. There is a great deal of wisdom to be gleaned from the observation of cats.

Once he caught a wasp, probably thinking it was just another fly in fancy dress off to a party or something, and it stung him on the lip. Then, to add insult to injury, it got away, buzzing round him insolently blowing raspberries and doing victory rolls and things before flying off into the sunset, never to be seen again. Whiskers let out a yell like a damned soul in torment and began to dance. He was very depressed for the next couple of days, and lurked under the sofa with a swollen face, looking at us as if it was all our fault. Another time he got hold of a huge moth and ate that. We could see that he didn't enjoy it, and I had the distinct impression, though he didn't actually say it, that he would really have preferred another wasp. I've never seen a more disgusted expression on the face of any other living creature than that of Whiskers when he discovered the taste of moth. He was pretty miserable after that experience, too, and he wisely left moths and wasps well alone for the rest of his days. Indeed, when a wasp happened to fly in through the window, Whiskers would get up from wherever he was sitting or lying and, with quiet dignity, firm step and an air of casual detachment, would leave the room, not returning until he was quite sure that the insect had gone. But he never lost his taste for a nice plump fly: I think for him they were a delicacy, like caviar.

He also had his preferences regarding liquid refreshment. I will not say he was a drinking cat, but he did have his likes. He loved a nice meat stock, even if we made it from a cube, though he did prefer the real thing, especially when it was cold and there was a thin layer of fat on the surface. He was not a great water drinker and was not particularly fond of tap water, although it's not bad round here, or bottled mineral water either, but from time to time he would binge on the goldfish water. Not that he did it often, as I say, but when he did, he did it in a big way, almost emptying the goldfish bowl with a greed which quite alarmed us. It quite alarmed the fish, too, who, judging by the expression on its face, was clearly wondering what was going to be his next move when all the water was finished. Shortly after, as can be easily imagined, the consequence was lots, but lots, of pee-pee, and we could see he was always a little shocked at, but also really rather proud of, the sheer copiousness of his output.

He was a very sensitive cat, as so many are, in direct contradiction to the wicked old myth, so often repeated, that cats are self-centred and without feelings. When one of us was ill or feeling depressed or low-spirited for some reason, we could always be sure that, sooner or later, there would be a little white paw against the leg and a sweet, friendly little face close to ours, accompanied by a consoling symphony of purrs and little squeaks. And there is no doubt: these small tender attentions invariably made us feel better almost immediately. Maybe the thing that was bothering you hadn't gone away, maybe the problem hadn't been solved, but you felt less alone in trying to solve it. A little warm, whiskery, purring solidarity from Whiskers the Cat had a kind of therapeutic, and even analgesic, quality all of its own. Or – let's be honest and say what we really mean – it had a kind of magic.

I'm not saying that only Whiskers had this quality. Many animals, dogs and cats in particular, have this sort of gift and are a quiet but constant blessing around the house, and this is a thing that we humans are, generally speaking, too slow to recognise and too mean about acknowledging and being grateful for; yet, after all, it is one of the great but beautifully simple things of life, and should remind us that Nature has provided not only for our material needs but, if we are disposed to reach out and take it, for our emotional needs as well.

Whiskers spent most of his youth and young adulthood half in the house and half out of it. He seemed divided right down the middle. Half of him was domesticated, sedentary, calm, rather sleepy. But the other half was all vagabond, outlaw, action cat. He loved roofs. When he went out he would often wander off and find his way, God knows how, up to the roofs of neighbouring houses – detached, semi-detached, terraces. We would often see him when we went shopping or out for a walk or whatever, strolling easily up and down somebody else's roof as if he owned the place, peeing briskly against their chimney-stacks, King of the Castle, Monarch of All He Surveyed, Lord of the Far Horizons.

Then there were plenty of other cats in the neighbourhood, and Whiskers, being a very sociable cat, had chums everywhere – and girlfriends as well. He was just over a year old when he began to frequent female company with a certain assiduousness – not to say half-crazed, goggle-eyed, feverish fanaticism. We'd brought him up well, and he became a fine big cat, tough as old leather and hard as nails, and generally speaking had very few real difficulties with the other males in the area who wanted to rassle with him for the favours of his female friends and acquaintances. This is not to say that he habitually went out looking for a scrap, though he was certainly not above it, but once he found himself embroiled in one he usually came off best and won, from the aforesaid females, the aforesaid favours, which they seemed to enjoy very much, and so did he and why not, because he had earned it.

He didn't, of course, win all the time – there were some other rough, tough fellows around those roofs of his – and he would often come home conspicuously bearing the signs of his victories, or defeats, on his person. It was in his ears that you could read his military history, because as the years passed they became gradually more – well, lacy, what with all the biting and scratching that went on. Once he was stuck in the house for nearly a month because of a bad bite on one of his paws which went septic, and we had to cram him with antibiotics, but he took it all rather philosophically, taking advantage of his temporary inactivity to preen and clean himself until his fur shone; when he was better he was soon back on his beat as if nothing had happened, and the gels were no doubt all delighted to have him back again, and they probably all partied and had a real good time.

His greatest friend/enemy/rival was a great big tough yellow cat that for some reason we called Hugo. He was probably a stray, or one of those semi-stray cats that have a base with some family but spend most of their time unshackled and free and without bonds of loyalty or affection. He had a rather neglected air, but we felt he must have had a steady income because he was robust and well-fed and self-assured, with an engaging, rapscallion, outlaw way about him that could turn to a chilling, feral ferocity when he got riled. He and Whiskers used to get along fine together most of the time, sunbathing in perfect amity on the roofs and climbing trees together, and we would often see them snoozing together on someone's roof or on top of a car, sometimes one using the other as a pillow and both purring loudly in enviable intimacy and harmony. I swear Whiskers sometimes invited him round to our place for dinner, and Hugo would stroll easily into the kitchen, tuck into Whiskers's bowl and then amble out again coolly, shoulder-to-shoulder with his chum. It was a great friendship to see, refined, courteous and civilised.

That is, till the gels turned up looking for a new boyfriend or even just a quick fling. Then that refined, courteous and civilised friendship went to hell and high water and stayed there for the duration. Clouds loured. Lightning flashed. Electricity was in the air and the time for living dangerously had come. All creation waited, tense, for the outcome.

Civilisation averted her gaze, Order withdrew the hem of her garment, the Rule of Law was suspended, and the deep jungle returned to impose its sway on the gardens and lawns and roofs of our quiet and respectable neighbourhood. Tyger Tyger burning bright/In the forests of the night . . . There were horrible screams and bestial feline oaths of the foulest and filthiest nature, and terrible physical clashes up the trees or on the roofs while the fair prize loitered nearby, awaiting the victor of this clash of furry Titans.

Sometimes Whiskers won. Sometimes Hugo won. They were so strong, so healthy, so well matched that the outcome could never be predicted with any confidence. But one thing is certain: whoever won, whoever lost, there were always going to be wounds to be dressed, claws and even teeth to be removed from some lacerated part, and ears, which with the passing of time resembled more and more some priceless product of the master lacemakers of Bruges, to be medicated.

Then, when the lady's scandalous and irresponsible lusts had been thoroughly assuaged (as things invariably turned out, by both of them – the fighting was always really about who was going to get first go), the old friendship between the two cats would slip back into gear and all the anger and rancour and madness of the war would be forgotten, and all the sins would be forgiven, and the insults would be dismissed with a casual, airy laugh, and the jungle would withdraw, and peace and tranquillity and law would return to the lawns and the gardens and the roofs. Until the next time. Until the next quavering female cry rose to the moon and certain scents carried on the breeze would set off the whole lunatic process all over again.

The friendship/enmity between Whiskers and Hugo lasted for quite a few years, ten or twelve if I remember rightly. Then, one day, Hugo just wasn't around any more. He'd gone. And Whiskers was clearly upset about it. We could see him looking for him. We could hear him calling out, up on the roofs, calling plaintively, clearly calling for him, but there was no answer.

Then one day, about three years after he'd disappeared, I saw Hugo again for the last time. He was under a bush in a garden not far from my house, and he'd clearly been on his travels, but he'd come back to the place of his youth and his wars and his victories and loves and defeats and his old friend. He seemed calm and happy to me, and I think he was happy to be back in his own place. I bent down to stroke him, and he purred a bit, but then I realised there was something wrong with him. He was paralysed. He couldn't move much, only his head and one of his forelegs. I went home and fetched him some chicken to eat, and I gave him some water with a spoon, and I think he enjoyed it. It was his last meal, because he died there, under that bush, shortly after he had finished it. I think he died happy, and without pain. But when I picked him up to take him away and bury him I realised – there was no mistaking the signs – that he had been hit by a car. Being old, he hadn't been able to get out of the way fast enough on the last stage of his journey home, maybe – who knows? – a journey back to see his old pal. I was so glad Whiskers hadn't seen him like that. It's silly, I know, but I was glad.

Hugo was Whiskers's best friend but he had plenty of other friends too, cats that turned up every so often, from heaven knows where, and would spend a few days roaming the gardens and the lanes and the roofs with Whiskers, and sometimes, in perfect amity, with Whiskers and Hugo as well. Those two did not have that dreadful and obsessive spirit of territoriality which is the curse of so many, though by no means all, tom-cats. They took things as they came, and most of the time they were sociable and hospitable. Indeed, on one memorable occasion, one of them – I think it was Whiskers but my wife says it was Hugo – stole a boiled chicken from an open saucepan on the kitchen table and carried it up to the flat roof of the garage. And there we saw them: Whiskers, who looked towards us every so often with an anxious and guilty air (not that it in any way inhibited his appetite, to tell the truth); Hugo, who occasionally flashed us what was clearly an ironic, somewhat mocking glance; and a third cat, whom we had never seen before. They were all working away at that boiled chicken with skill, energy and verve, and, be it said, with a certain haste too, as if they were scared I just might get hold of a ladder and come yelling up to claim my lunch back. My own belief is that they stole the chicken not only because they liked chicken and saw their chance to grab one (as they say, it is the opportunity that makes the thief), but also in order to feast a distinguished guest. Naturally, we were a bit annoyed about the chicken, but they really were so funny, those three rascals up there working away with a will on a chicken they knew was not theirs, before the very eyes of its legitimate proprietors, that all we could do was laugh.

Whiskers, naturally, got a good scolding when he came back home later, much later, with slow, repentant steps and a lowered head and ears penitentially flattened against his head. He seemed very sad and sorry, but there was just something, a smug something, in his eyes that told me that, under the surface, he was sure it had been worth it.

When I got up the next morning I saw Hugo, sitting outside on the kitchen window-ledge and staring into the kitchen – staring, in particular, towards the saucepans. I was glad the window was closed: he had a lurking, suspicious, vaguely criminal air about him. He had enjoyed that chicken, no question of that, and he was hanging around clearly hoping to get hold of another one. When I gave him a severe, reproachful, 'How could you do this to me, you wicked ungrateful cat?' look, he licked his lips and actually grinned at me. Then, with dignity, he jumped down and went off to join Whiskers somewhere, his nose and tail in the air.

From time to time Whiskers would bring us home a little present. Birds. Bats. Once a field mouse. Once even a lizard, and God only knows where he got that. He invariably brought them in with an air of absolute pride and achievement, clearly believing that he fully deserved not only our praise but our undying gratitude into the bargain. Well, maybe he did – I'm not saying he didn't – but he certainly didn't get it. Quite the opposite. We received his small gifts with screams and screeches and yells of disgust and, in the case of the bats, fear. Everyone in my family, myself included, is terrified of bats, and none of us would ever, under any circumstances, keep one as a pet, so we could never understand why Whiskers insisted on bringing us the creatures. Maybe it was his sense of humour. If so, he had a very odd one. In any case, our reactions, which he probably considered out of place, foolish and exaggerated, never managed to discourage him. Right up until he started losing his teeth with age, these little trophies of his would arrive regularly on our kitchen floor, with Whiskers staring up at us, willing us to praise him and always surprised and hurt when we wouldn't. He was nothing if not constant.

And one day he brought us quite a different present. We never found out where he got it from, but he brought us home a tiny little tabby kitten not much bigger than a can of beans and screaming like a mad thing. He brought it right up to me, of course, holding it by the scruff of the neck just like the mother cats do, and he popped it into my lap with an exhausted air and an expression on that face of his that meant something along the lines of 'I've done my bit and I'm shattered. Now the rest is up to you. I'm going for a beer, if that's all right by you.' Or words to that effect. Then he crawled off somewhere and made himself scarce, leaving me holding the baby.

I was – well, disconcerted. I mean to say! I mean, what do you do when a male cat brings you a kitten home, a kitten that looks as if it's just not going to make it without its mum around? And where was Whiskers? What was he doing? Was this a kidnapping case? Was Whiskers, even now, writing the ransom note? What would I get for kitnapping? Ignorance is not an excuse in the eyes of the law, or so I've been told.

We did the only thing we could do with that kitten. That is, we adopted it. My daughter was absolutely delighted. She immediately transformed herself into a substitute mother – a very efficient substitute mother; the original couldn't have done any better herself – and nourished the newcomer lovingly with her doll's feeding bottle, and that newcomer certainly enjoyed getting nourished and drank gallons of choice Jersey milk. She survived. I don't know about the Jersey cows, but she survived and became Cat Number 2 in our ménage, and lived a long and happy and, I am sorry to say, from time to time extremely immoral life in the bosom of our family.

Once he had successfully got her inserted into the household, Whiskers showed very great indifference towards our new family member. I felt this was rather unkind of him since he had lumbered us with her, and I thought he might at least play with her a bit from time to time. Once in a while he would stroll casually up to her and give her a quick cursory sniff, checking she was all right and that we were doing our duty by her, then off he would go. We had the job of looking after her, and he was just making sure we were keeping up to scratch, supervising us.

I've often wondered what can have induced a male cat to do that. I think that on his wanderings on the roofs or in the backyards or lanes and ditches he had found the little creature abandoned and starving and had spontaneously done something that would have been logical and natural, indeed a moral imperative, in a human being. He'd picked it up and carried it to safety. In other words, whichever way you look at it, he had carried out an act of charity and altruism and generosity. He'd saved the life of one of his own kind, and the funny thing is that when he brought the kitten in there was none of the rolling about and preening and showing off and exhibitionism that he laid on for us when he brought back a mouse or a bat or a bird. In conclusion, it's quite clear to me that dogs and cats are not just driven by survival instincts and looking after Number One, but they are also influenced by emotional drives. Whiskers and Hugo, except in those insane moments when the purely animal instincts got the upper hand, really were friends. Whiskers brought that kitten home because he wanted to help it, he wanted to save its life, and he knew how that was done – bring it back to the boss. And cats stay with people because they give them food and shelter, but also because they give them the emotional nourishment that is so obviously one of their basic needs. The thing, by the way, is reciprocal. We like to have cats and dogs around us because we need to give affection and to get affection back. We need them. We need them because they teach us. They teach us to love and value creatures other than those of our own species and, by extension, or at least this seems to me to be the logical conclusion, they teach us to love and value the world itself. They're a bridge between what is exclusively human and the rest of creation, and if we didn't have that bridge, what sort of relationship would we have with all the rest? It doesn't bear thinking about. With them, we're part of a chain. Without them, we'd be on our own, all six billion of us – but six billion what?

The kitten grew up into a rather lovely little cat. She was always much smaller than the average cat – we used to say she was pocket-sized – and she was of a rather unpredictable nature, like the English weather. Sometimes she'd be unbelievably sweet and affectionate and outgoing, other times touchy and sulky and fussy. She and Whiskers became good friends, and, I have to say, from time to time lovers, producing a fair number of kittens between them as the years passed. The usual package was two black-and-white kittens, just like Dad, two tabbies, just like Mum, and, to make a bunch of five, a Siamese. Now that was weird, but that's the way it went when those two had been intimate. The tip of her tail was a bit twisted, but that cat was the classic tabby, with the unmistakable dark blot on the roof of her mouth which is what you should look for if you are a connoisseur of tabbies. A vet once told me (without knowing about the fifth kittens, as a matter of fact) that the little twist in the tail probably meant her father had been a Siamese. So there you are. As the reader may or may not have guessed, this cat was none other than Tibby, the noble heroine whose latter years I have already discussed in some detail.

Some cultures believe that cats have nine lives. Others, less generous, or perhaps less observant and therefore unaware of the vast potential and innumerable talents of cats, allow them around seven. Most cultures, however, agree that cats are endowed with more lives than the ordinary mortal such as ourselves and one more than the Devil. It is my firm opinion, much of which is based on the example of Whiskers, that they do indeed have at least nine lives, but probably even more in particular cases. And Whiskers, it must be said, made the most of every single one of his, right up to the final one. He was a cat who often ended up in one kind of a fix or another, sometimes through no fault of his own and other times very much his own fault. When he was still a kitten he caught one of those nasty chills, accompanied by a terrible cough and a lot of vomiting from one extremity and diarrhoea from the other because it seems that he had lost (it is not clear how or where) what the vets call his intestinal flora. For a few days it looked as though we were about to lose yet another cat, and an atmosphere of gloom hung over the household, influencing, I believe, the goldfish and the turtle as well as the human components of the family. But we looked after him and we gave him his medicines and we cleaned him and fed him and fanned him and, imperceptibly at first but then more obviously, he began to recover. He was too weak to wash himself, so once he started looking clearly better it fell to me to give him the occasional bath. He was completely drained and clearly in a state of terror, and he weighed no more than a woolly sock the first time I gave him his bath. I didn't really want to do it, but he was in such a mess that it had to be done. He bit my thumb. It was the first and last time he ever bit any of us. And I have to say that, tiny and weak as he was, he packed one hell of a bite: his teeth went in good and deep and they hurt like hell. I've still got the scar. I can see it now as I write. But the thing that sticks most in my mind was how sorry I felt for him. That bite was the gesture of a sick and desperate little creature giving way to blind panic; there was no rage in it, or nastiness, but just sheer, blind, irrational terror, and a terrified animal is a dreadful thing to see.

Another time he miscalculated while going after a bluebottle and took a flying leap out of an upstairs window. It was a bad mistake, and would certainly have put a premature end to his career if he had not had the presence of mind to catch at an edge of curtain that just happened to be sticking out of the downstairs window immediately underneath the one he had chosen to leave so precipitously and unconventionally. He ended up swinging about two centimetres above the concrete flagstones that had been waiting, in the sullen and obdurate manner of concrete flagstones, to receive him. You could almost see him going 'Whew' as he clearly realised he had just cashed in one of those nine lives of his for a missed rugby tackle at a bluebottle, of all things. However, as they say, a miss is as good as a mile. He looked very silly. His reputation for intelligence was badly compromised and it took a great deal before he regained it. But at least he had saved his hide. Afterwards, he was not very well for a while, the one and only time I have seen a cat who was actually sick, and copiously sick into the bargain, with fear. In fact, he had scared himself silly. And he kept a low profile for a few days afterwards, as if he didn't want us to remind him of such an unheard-of and clamorous loss of feline face. I mean, what cat worth the name chucks himself out of windows?

Then there was the time a friend of ours came round for a visit, asking if he could bring his dog along because he didn't like to leave it alone in his flat. I checked that Whiskers was out – not that I'd actually ever seen how he reacted to dogs, since he spent most of his time out on the roofs and up the trees, but I thought he might not get on very well with them.

Well, our friend turned up with this great massive black Alsatian, as big as a wolf and built like a rhinoceros. And he had a set of monumental white teeth that sent shivers down your spine just to look at them, just to know they were there in the same room with you. He stretched himself down on the carpet, perfectly tranquil and calm, with a tongue about a foot long lolling out of his mouth and dribbling saliva rhythmically every three seconds. He was – well, a disconcerting thing to see, especially that close. I mean, he would have been all right in a zoo, behind bars and everything, but here he was just a bit overwhelming.

Suddenly, while we were chatting and sipping our beers, the dog leapt to his feet with a long roar, not loud but deep and vibrant and very scary, in his massive throat, which (I am not exaggerating) was as solid as a log of oak. He had seen Whiskers.

Whiskers was home. Whiskers had not gone out. In fact, he had gone for a little snooze in the half-open drawer of a wardrobe, hidden in a pile of pullovers – I found the little nest he had made for himself later on.

Then Whiskers saw him.

Whiskers came down the passageway with his eyes fixed on the intruder, every hair on his body on end and his tail high in the air and puffed out so much he made me think of a peacock, though he looked nothing like a peacock. He looked three times his usual size and he looked mean. The dog watched him. Whiskers moved towards him in incredible slow motion, placing one paw slowly in front of the other with great precision and great determination and great concentration, and the message he gave out was something like, 'Now I'm coming in and there's nothing in the world can stop me, okay, you big lump of whatever you are! And my advice to you is, git!'

The dog just stared at him, his head on one side, his nose working, a bit perplexed, a bit curious, and certainly a bit amused as well. Whiskers stopped about half a metre from him, stared him right in the eyes, stood on tiptoe to make himself as tall as he could, then came out with a long, shrill, wavering scream, full of outrage, of defiance, of contempt.

For quite some time the dog gave no reaction at all. He just stared at this small, odd, audacious black-and-white thing, almost in disbelief. Then he moved his head forward, with immense grace, until their two noses were practically touching, and simply said, 'Bow!'

It was a splendid 'Bow!', not loud, but compelling, deep bass, sonorous, resonant, dignified, decisive. Whiskers, mouth gaping, held his gaze for about ten long seconds, and then simply keeled over in a heap. He had fainted.

I am told cats do not faint. Well, that is as it may be, but my cat fainted. I think it was that mechanism which is set off in animals when they realise the predator has got them and their number is up. They become paralysed and fall into a catatonic state or a sort of coma, this being, I think, a merciful boon on the part of Mother Nature, so that they do not feel anything when they are getting – well, eaten. Whiskers, maybe for the first and last time in his life, had felt himself to be in the condition not of the hunter, the predator, but of the victim, the prey, and he had reacted like one of his own victims. But, thinking about it, thinking of that great dark wolfish muzzle, those monstrous fangs and the absolute determination in that 'Bow!', I'm pretty sure that, in the same situation, I'd have fainted too.

The Alsatian, his gentle rebuke having had the desired effect, settled back down on the floor, cool and phlegmatic, let his tongue loll out as before, and went back to his pacific and soothing pastime of salivating all over my carpet.

I scooped up Whiskers, inert and lifeless, bore him aloft and locked him in the bedroom. He was still out for the count and remained so for a good half hour at least. As I was carrying him I felt how boneless he had become: it was like carrying a damp towel. There wasn't a single tense muscle or tendon in his body, and his fur was still all puffed up and incredibly soft to the touch. I let him sleep. And when he did come to his senses again his eyes were big and round as saucers and he looked basically stoned. He must have been on an adrenalin high, as the saying goes. The dog was gone by then, with his master, home to his dinner, but it took quite a while before Whiskers plucked up enough courage to go back into the sitting room. He would loiter at the far end of the hallway and peer in to see if the *whatever it was* was still there. He got over it, of course, but I believe that, for the rest of his life, he was never really sure if what had happened had actually happened, or if it hadn't just been a pretty spectacular nightmare. Because cats have nightmares too.

For us, going on holiday was always a bit of a problem. First there was the problem about what to do with Whiskers while we were away. Then there was the problem of what to do with Whiskers and Tibby while we were away. Then there was the problem of what to do about Whiskers and Tibby and Manfred and Willy and Olga and Lucy and Flea and Ronald and – well, the list is endless, to say nothing of the goldfish and the turtle who, having once arrived in our ménage for one reason or another had found it to their liking and made plain their intention of staying put unless forcibly evicted by the bailiffs. The turtle nominally belonged to a friend of ours, but *de facto* he gradually became ours, as much as a turtle can be anybody's. The thing didn't bother me. He would never be the life and soul of any party, that turtle, but I rather liked him, though my wife put up with him but basically couldn't stand him.

Once we sent Whiskers to a cat hotel, or I should say Cat Hotel, because it had all of five stars, self-awarded I believe. It was quite a nice place, in the hills, and there were plenty of other nice cats there who, the owner assured us, would be great company for Whiskers while we were away. He would have a whale of a time, and the only problem, he assured us, would be convincing Whiskers to come home with us after having savoured all the delights this exemplary retreat had to offer to even the most difficult and demanding of cats.

We went off for three weeks, and we had, for the record, a lovely holiday, but of course the first thing we did when we got back (which, as it happened, was a day earlier than we had agreed with the hotel) was to drive along to pick up Whiskers and bring him back to the bosom of his family.

Things had gone rather badly. When we arrived at the hotel, we found that Whiskers was not with the other cats. He had been shut in the attic. He had been segregated. The hotel owner explained to us that Whiskers had not behaved himself very well. In fact, he had behaved himself very badly, squabbling and quarrelling and arguing with the other cats most of the time. He had refused to take part in their games and group activities. He had stolen their things and hidden them. He had behaved badly with the hotel owner and his wife. He had been sullen and huffy and non-cooperative.

The hotel owner was extremely indignant. He seemed to think that we had deliberately landed him with a feline sociopath with grave attitude problems, a delinquent of the very worst sort, and he declared in an extremely aggrieved tone that the fee we had already agreed upon was not even remotely enough to compensate him for all he had had to go through. He gave us the clear impression that, for him, Whiskers was a sort of bloodthirsty monster, a devil incarnate, a feline nightmare. Then he took us up to the attic.

They had shut him in a cage in a dark, dusty loft and he was nothing but skin and bones – they told us he had refused to eat anything from the day he had arrived. The place stank, and he was crouched in a corner of the cage half-asleep and the living image of unhappiness, loneliness and neglect.

As soon as he saw us he leapt to his feet with a long, loud cry, making sure that we knew that he had recognised us, and there was such anguish in that cry, and suffering, and joy and relief. It was at one and the same time a reproach and a greeting and a welcome. When I picked him up – and he was so light – he started purring loudly, and he licked my face from my temples to my chin with acute little whining sounds of pure happiness. Let no one ever tell me cats have no feelings.

The hotel people were flabbergasted. They had suddenly realised that Whiskers's delinquency had nothing to do with some innate wickedness, but had everything to do with homesickness and grief, with missing the people and places he needed so much. It had everything to do with love.

We paid the fee we had agreed upon without any argument, and as we drove away it was with a certain feeling of rage and resentment, but also with a sense of satisfaction: the air of shame and mortification that hung about those two individuals in part compensated us for the unfeeling way they had treated our poor cat.

Needless to say, that was the last time we left any cat of ours in one of those cat hotel places. Not for this, by the way, am I damning the category, and I am sure that there are plenty of places of this sort that are above reproach. But, as the saying goes, once bitten, twice shy. In one way or another, since then we have always managed to find a way to leave our cats at home when we've gone away, with regular visits from somebody they know and full liberty to maintain their usual rhythms and routines and normal daily life.

Like so many cats, Whiskers had a double life, and maybe a triple and a quadruple one and so on. We know of our cats only what it pleases them, in their infinite goodness, to let us know, but a large part of their lives, and certainly the part they live outside, is secret and intimate and their own exclusive property.

Whiskers had another base, another human centre in his life – we were not the only ones. He used to visit an old unmarried lady, living in a street not far from ours, who kept him well supplied with tasty titbits and milk and little savoury treats. He even had his own little basket in her house, though she knew perfectly well he wasn't her cat, just for when he felt like having a little snooze. We only found out about her some considerable time, years indeed, after their relationship (as it were) had begun; it seems that he used to drop by at least two or three times a week, and sometimes much more often, for many years, and they, and indeed we, in due course became very good friends.

It just happened that one day the old lady, who had no idea who Whiskers belonged to, was passing by and she saw him sitting, half-snoozing and sunning himself, on our window-ledge. I happened to be looking out of the window myself at the time and I saw her glance towards our house, then give a little double-take full of surprise and pleasure. Then she said, 'Oh! Mickey!' and gave a little wave, and Whiskers woke up, looked in her direction and came out with a little miaow! of greeting and pleasure. He got up on his feet and arched his back and stretched, and started purring away contentedly as he gazed with friendly eyes at the old lady.

'Mickey!' she said again. 'And how are you? I haven't seen you since Tuesday!' and Whiskers purred even louder than before and started rolling around on the window-ledge. Then the old lady saw me through the window and gave a rather embarrassed little smile, and with a 'Bye, Mickey!' off she went briskly down the road.

I eyed Whiskers. 'Mickey?' I said. Whiskers, to his credit, be it said, had the grace to look a little embarrassed too.

I was speechless. Mickey. Whiskers had another name. An alias! Whiskers Also Known As, as the papers say. Whiskers AKA. Whiskers alias Mickey.

I met the old lady in the street a few days later. We greeted each other with a rather strained formality, and I was continuing on my way when she stopped me by asking, 'And how's Mickey?'

'Oh, fine, fine,' I said airily and somewhat coldly. I was jealous.

She wasn't cowed or discouraged by any means. 'Oh, we're great friends, you know. He's always coming round to see me. What a handsome cat! And so good-natured. And so full of life!'

I began to unbend. A person who was able to recognise the manifold virtues of our splendid cat could only be a good person, a valid person, a positive person, a friend. And so a good and firm friendship began between me and the old lady which was to last many years, and when we met in the street we would always stop and discuss all the latest deeds and doings

202

of our – well, our mutual cat. It was an easy, urbane friendship, yet solid and enduring, and it gave me a rather delightful alternative perspective on Whiskers and a little glimpse into the sort of things he did in his life – or one of his lives – beyond our garden hedges.

When my daughter was nine years old and Whiskers was seven, we had another child, a little boy, and Tibby gave birth to several kittens at more or less the same time. It was quite an amusing sight to see the two mothers on the sofa, my wife at one end and Tibby at the other, feeding their offspring together.

Whiskers had no problem with the baby, but he couldn't stand the kittens. Whenever we tried to put one of them near him he would get up and stride off with an offended, rather disgusted air. He was not what one would call a model father.

But he was extremely interested in the baby and would often hang around the cradle, staring in. When the baby started crawling around a bit he followed it everywhere, observing everything it did with great curiosity. In some ways Whiskers was rather a confused cat, and it was clear he felt himself much more father to the baby than to the kittens. Well, that was just as well, because we gave every kitten in that batch away as soon as they were weaned. We didn't really feel like coping with a new-born baby and an entire club of very lively and very active kittens at one and the same time. But we had no difficulty in giving them away, of course – they were pretty spectacular kittens, and overflowing with fun and good nature.

We knew that Whiskers had certain female associates – and they were not only human – outside the house, as well as enjoying the (let's tell the truth) enthusiastic favours of Tibby in the peace and tranquillity of his domestic sphere. One day the old lady told me about one of Whiskers's/Mickey's deeds – because she always called him Mickey and I always called him Whiskers and we quite happily agreed to differ – concerning his extra-marital liaisons.

Near the old lady's house there was an enormous old abandoned building, several hundreds of years old in fact, which in the glorious centuries of its heyday had been a coaching inn and for long afterwards had been relegated to the modest but not unworthy role of being one of the several local pubs. It was a most suggestive and picturesque old place even in its ruin, ivy-covered, with steep roofs and tall chimney-stacks and most marvellous windows and time-weathered black-and-yellow brickwork. I know that many people were tempted to buy it, and to try to restore it to some of its former splendour as a fine and dignified old building that represented a considerable part of our local history, but that was a daunting and expensive task – or, to be honest, a very daunting and a very expensive task indeed.

As the months and the years and the decades passed, the old building became more and more abandoned and more decrepit, but it never quite became an eyesore, being intrinsically most charming and dignified and beautiful even in a state of neglect and decay. And, naturally, it was a paradise, or maybe a thieves' kitchen is a more accurate term, for cats.

For me – but I am prejudiced – this was its finest hour. It became the centre for a merry band of stray cats of all shapes and sizes and races and creeds, tiny kittens just starting out on life's journey, robust, swashbuckling, devil-may-care toms with their somewhat inconstant molls, anxious mums and squabbling siblings, serene and grizzled oldies sunning themselves at the porch or lounging around washing their paws under the ivy, and the very old awaiting in calm dignity the Tap On The Shoulder that would tell them their time was up. And they were all, it seems, friends, or at any rate acquaintances, of Whiskers. It was a sort of Court of Miracles, with cats old and young all living together in precarious harmony. And I know some of the older people in the neighbourhood used to bring them something to eat every day. We ourselves made our own contribution from time to time, as did friends of ours, and I think the mousing opportunities were rather good round there too, so although it cannot be said that they were living in the lap of luxury, those cats didn't do too badly for themselves. At least they enjoyed a good five of the essential things that make the difference between mere survival and quality of life: freedom, food, security, shelter and the company of their kind. And then, of course, they could also enjoy the not-infrequent society of cats from, let us say, the more respectable parts of town.

At last, however, the inevitable happened, and their idyllic, if occasionally riotous, Robin Hood outlaw life had to come to an end. Somebody smart enough to realise its immense potential value as well as its breathtaking beauty, and courageous enough to decide to take the risk, bought the property with the aim of bringing it back to life again. And, of course, the first step in this otherwise highly praiseworthy project was, well, to evict the cats, most certainly to their great grief. And no doubt also to the grief of many of the old folks in the area who, in their unobtrusive way, had been looking after them, and who had felt that this was a worthy and charitable task to be doing, a task which also kept them out and about and on the go and was a meaningful and happy and enriching alternative to sitting monotonously on the sofa guzzling snacks and dozily and passively watching television half the day. The new owners contacted a voluntary organisation involved in animal welfare. They sent an expert and experienced team along, with food, laced with a pretty potent sleep-inducing agent, which they left in a big sort of trough just in front of the porch. Naturally, all the cats, young and old, gathered gleefully round this un-expected and extremely tasty banquet, thinking it was Christmas or something, and, fearing no treason as the saying goes, got their little muzzles down and tucked in. One by one they collapsed, and the old lady watched as the animal welfare people picked them up one after the other and gently tucked them into little cages in their van.

Everything was going just fine and dandy when Whiskers arrived on the scene of the round-up. The old lady was just about to shout from her window that Whiskers was not one of the strays but a respect-able animal with a wife and job and home and family when a very strange thing happened. One of the cats still on its feet – though staggering about drunkenly as the tranquilliser took effect – was Whiskers's current fiancée, a sweet neat little creature, grey and white with unexpectedly, dramatically, black forepaws. Whiskers, who was nobody's fool, took in the situation at a glance and sprang into action. He raced towards his fiancée, swelled up his chest, danced around her to attract her undivided attention, made little barking noises, and then began to push her, with his head, towards the ivy-covered wall which separated the grounds of the old inn from the adjacent property. She, half-asleep, protested weakly but obeyed, and when they arrived at the wall, Whiskers, with his head and his paws, with blows and head-butts, forced her, already nearly senseless, to drag herself up the ivy. Once they reached the top of the wall Whiskers pushed her unceremoniously down the other side, and both of them disappeared into the bushes.

Whiskers's fiancée was the only cat to escape the Great Cat Round-Up. All the others were taken away by the animal-lovers. We never did find out what actually happened to them, but I am sure it would have been very hard to find, for them, a valid substitute for their grand old life of anarchic liberty in one of the ancient coaching inns of England. For myself and other like-minded people, while we welcomed and applauded the restoration of the wonderful old building, it was, at the very least, as though an important aspect of our locality, something odd but unique, half-comical, half-poetical and in its way intensely meaningful, had been taken away from us, and a small but somehow necessary part of our lives and our identities had been obliterated. I admire what the restorers did, and I have nothing but praise for them – the old inn is once again what it was, or even better than it was, in its days of glory – but as I pass it of an evening just as the twilight is coming down I seem sometimes to see lots of little shadows, or little ghosts, wandering around bewildered in the dusk and trying to get back in. A spirit of sorrow or depression or melancholy settles on me for a bit, until I shake it off and bow humbly to the fact that we all have our exits and our entrances but that life itself goes on. The old lady herself adopted Whiskers's fiancée so, at least for her, life went on and things turned out all right, because she could not have found a better or sweeter mistress. And, naturally enough and as was right and proper, Whiskers became a sort of hero, a sort of knight errant, a paladin, a Bayard without fear and without reproach for all the old ladies of the area. I remember one of them saying to me with accusatory eyes, as if I had done something to her: 'If only men were like him!' It made me squirm a bit, but I knew what she meant.

Time stands still for nobody, and it did not make an exception even for Whiskers the Cat. For a good ten years or so he was the uncontested boss of the roofs and gardens of our part of town. Every so often he had to accept some minor setback, above all in his squabbles with Hugo when some female was involved, but usually he won his battles, and even if he did come home from time to time with a few more bites and scratches and scars he also carried himself with an air of self-confidence and sheer toughness that more than convinced us that his life as warrior and ladykiller was still going strong.

But time won't stand still, not even for the great warriors and ladykillers and knights in shining armour. As he got older, Whiskers started losing his battles and coming home with cuts and wounds that were not the light and negligible things of his heyday. New cats were turning up in the area, younger, tougher, more aggressive, and it was clear they were a bit more than our old pal could handle. He got roughed up quite a lot, and some of his wounds were pretty serious and needed the vet. He also got obsessed with defending his territory and he stayed out for ages, alert, on guard, defending a kingdom which, in reality, he had already lost – lost to time, lost to the younger generation, as is, in her wisdom, Nature's way. He got skinnier and shabbier, no longer the proud and happy cat of his prime and his maturity, wandering around with an air that was at one and the same time defiant and profoundly bewildered. When he fought, it was no longer with that old self-confidence of his but with a sort of miserable tenacity which could not conceal the fact that it was almost certain by now that he was fighting because it was in him to fight and not because he wanted to fight: fighting to lose, fighting to yield ground, not to defend it or gain it, fighting to see some new and vigorous upstart win this or that roof, this or that garden, this or that female.

He came home limping and bloody one day, with a long, deep cut on his neck and one of his ears in shreds and the marks of a savage bite on one of his paws. And it was clear that the wounds in his spirit went far deeper than the ones on his body, an old King of the Castle coming to realise that the moment of his abdication had come.

The vet kept him in his clinic for a good ten days, cleaned up his cuts and wounds and got rid of the infections and the parasites that had come to him as a consequence of them and of the psychological and physical state he had fallen into. Then he became quite grave and serious and gave us a good talking-to. He told us Whiskers was undernourished and very weak, and that we were going to lose him if we didn't decide on a radical step. He said we should get him doctored – castrated, that is – if we wanted him to get his tranquillity back, if we wanted to give him another few years of serenity and contentment and peace.

I was taken aback, to be honest. For me, an important part of Whiskers had always been the outlaw, the womaniser, the warrior, that part of him that was so much in contrast with his domestic identity, what we saw of him at home. But my wife and I discussed it, and we discussed it with the kids too, and we came to the conclusion that the vet was right.

He was pretty clear and made no bones about it. 'If he goes on like this,' he told us, 'there's no two ways about it, he'll die. That's the way he's made. He'll never give up fighting – he can't, it isn't in him – and one of those cats out there will kill him. There's no doubt about it. And it's a shame,' he said, caressing Whiskers's poor, battered, tattered, sleeping head, 'because he's got plenty of years left in him. Do it.

Let's get this operation done and you'll see the difference at once.'

Okay. We trusted him. He was our friend. We did it. After ten days we brought Whiskers home, skinny and weak and the shadow of what he used to be. We kept our fingers crossed, hoping that, as the vet had said, the operation would bring about a change for the better.

The most immediate consequence of the operation was that Whiskers stayed at home a lot more. Very occasionally he popped out to check his roofs and gardens, but he avoided any contact with the new robber barons who had muscled in on his territory. From time to time heroic and Homeric struggles could be heard and seen on the roofs and in the gardens and down the lanes and in the bushes, but Whiskers, although sometimes he seemed a bit curious and even a bit nostalgic for the good old fighting days, wisely decided to keep himself well out of them.

He began to fatten up a bit. His appetite came back – it came back with a vengeance, to tell the truth – and before a couple of weeks had passed he was looking like another cat, rejuvenated, nearly his handsome old self once again. And his old joyous, playful spirit came back too, and soon he was playing with the children again, and with us, and with the other cats in the family. He went back to his old hobby of collecting things and hiding them under the furniture, an activity that he had suspended during his long years of war and passion. There was a new peace and serenity in him, something that he transmitted to our children, who treated him with the greatest sweetness, consideration and respect.

Every so often we used to hear of the Chinese authorities ordering the cats and dogs to be massacred, saying they were parasites who did nothing but consume, taking without giving. Nothing could be more fatuous. Nothing could be farther from the truth. We have already seen how they can freely give affection and love and happiness, but perhaps what is even more important is that they really do teach children to love and care for other creatures, and also for themselves. When children feel that their affection for an animal is returned, when they feel that their caresses are appreciated, that their little treats are received with joy, they feel more important, they feel wanted, they feel loved, and no one can calculate how much the love of an animal contributes to a child's self-confidence and self-esteem.

Whiskers, from the very first day we brought him home, had always been a most affectionate, outgoing and grateful cat, even when his mind was preoccupied with other, feline problems. But in his latter years, with the serenity of his new tenor of life, he became much more so. For all of us it was a joy to come home from work or from school to find him sprawled along the carpet or stretched out on the sofa, to hear his little welcoming miaow, and then to hear all the purring starting up like a solid little motor.

He became a fine, plump, healthy cat with a beautiful shiny coat and a relaxed air, *a gravitas* that was a long, long way from his old swashbuckling, death-defying air of yesteryear. He liked to spend his time snoozing on someone's lap, playing, eating – lots – and every so often he would pop out to see how his old manor was getting on, but scrupulously avoiding hostilities. He had his little habits and routines. He was always there to accompany my son to bed. He always had a little snooze on my bed in the mornings in the warm place I left after I had got up. Every evening, at more or less the same hour, he would sip a little water from the goldfish bowl, and we used to say it was Whiskers's teatime. When he did go out in the evenings he would be back at eight o'clock on the dot – and I know nobody is going to believe this, but he came back at eight o'clock precisely even when the clocks changed to summer time. I suspect he was probably unconsciously guided by the church bells, otherwise I have no explanation for this; I mean, we hadn't bought him a watch or anything. And, of course, he regularly popped in to visit his old friend and his ex-fiancée, with whom he now maintained a strictly Platonic relationship of course, and enjoyed a little snack and a little civilised conversation with them.

He started losing his teeth. There was nothing particularly dramatic about it, just that from time to time one of us would notice that a tooth was missing here, and another there, but he never lost his appetite or his innate, characteristic good nature. We all loved him, and so did all our friends, because he was a fine, handsome, friendly cat and his basic goodness of spirit was apparent to all. Only one of my friends, in all the years that we had him, actually disliked him – he disliked cats in general and he was one of those people who despise any show of affection towards an animal. When Whiskers would amble up to him, expecting some brief gesture of friendliness and goodwill, he would be rudely snubbed for his pains.

Whiskers was getting on in years, a bit senile maybe, but he was never a cat who tolerated being snubbed and he was not the type of animal you ignored with impunity. One day he clearly made up his mind that enough was enough and that he was going to have to show this pal of ours, whatever he thought he was, that he couldn't come into our house, into his house, and treat a bright and sensitive creature like him in this cavalier manner. And even in the autumn of his life, when Whiskers decided he was going to do something he went and did it, without so much as a by your leave. Maybe he brooded, maybe he bided his time, but when the opportunity arose the thing got done.

It was winter, and this friend of ours had come round to give me a hand with an urgent job of work of the sort that has to be finished by yesterday. He arrived with a rather fancy hat, a splendid tweed overcoat, a nice cashmere scarf and a wonderful pair of sheepskin gloves. He took all these garments off and lined them up neatly on the sofa. Then he came across to me at my desk and we started working.

Whiskers came ambling in. He gave me his customary miaow! or rather miaow? of greeting, the interrogative tone intended to elicit the usual 'Hi, Whiskers, how's tricks?' or similar from me, which he duly got. He did the same to my friend and he got the usual predictable cold shoulder for his pains.

It was an error. A fatal error. Whiskers had clearly been brooding for months, biding his time, and now an unrepeatable opportunity had presented itself. It was now or never. Whiskers decided it was going to be now, and never mind the consequences. He stared my friend in the eye, actually out-staring him, then turned on his heel, strolled across the room, leapt up on to the sofa and then, one after the other, peed a little on everything he found there, hat, overcoat, scarf, glove and glove. Then he jumped back down and strolled off to bed with his tail in the air; and if cats can laugh, and I think they can inside themselves, he was laughing his head off. Not perhaps the most sophisticated of revenges, but a hit, a palpable hit.

All things must pass. This is in the very laws of existence and there is nothing we can do about it. Even all beautiful things must pass, in spite of all the strenuous efforts of our poets and our artists to preserve them. But pure beauty in itself is worth so very much that sometimes it seems that sheer infinity is nothing, absolutely nothing, in comparison. Or perhaps real beauty actually is the intuition of the infinite. And there is nothing more beautiful than pure, spontaneous and disinterested love. It really is an immense privilege, to love and to be loved. And it is an enormous privilege to know, as human beings, that animals, too, have this capacity to love and to be loved. Humankind is not alone in the universe – the animals are with us.

I used to take my little son to a small park near our home in the afternoons, where he could spend two or three hours with his chums, playing anything from football to tig or whatever other game was in fashion with them at any given time.

We went there, as usual, one afternoon in August, and we got back home around half past six in the evening – a bit early for August, really, because normally when the weather was decent we'd stay out till eight or even later.

When we got back home, I remember, I was just pulling my key out of the lock when we heard this strange sort of lamenting cry that was coming from my daughter's bedroom.

We went in and we heard the cry again. It was coming from under the bed. It was coming from Whiskers. I recognised that cry. I'd heard it only two or three times before, but I knew exactly what it was. There is a sort of cry that, if he makes it, a cat will make only once in his life, like the legendary song of the swan. When a cat is very old – and Whiskers was about fifteen, which is a very good age for the average cat – it's as if, at a certain point, something just gives in him. Something yields, or sort of breaks

219

down. Maybe it's a form of heart attack or a stroke but, in any case, it's fatal. After it happens, the cat might live just a little longer, two or three weeks, especially if the vet gives him a hand, but once it's happened there's no appeal, the game's up and it's only a question of time. The cat's dying, and that's it. And it is then, and only then, that you hear that strange and rare cry, shrill, helpless, full of bewilderment and curiosity. The cat doesn't know what has happened to him, but he knows it is something much bigger than he can handle. And it is then that he tries to dig himself in somewhere, to hide, to take his distance from things.

Whiskers was under my daughter's bed. I believe he had suffered something along the lines of a massive stroke while we were out and his hind quarters were paralysed – his legs couldn't move and his tail couldn't move – and when I saw him I could see, with an acute sense of shock, the writing on the wall: Whiskers was about to leave us.

Of course, we were not unprepared for this. I had tried to forewarn the kids. We all knew that Whiskers, in cat terms, was a pretty old cat and we couldn't really hope that he would last that much longer: that's Nature. But, as we all know, there's a huge difference between knowing a thing and seeing it happen, between idea and reality. There's a great big difference between idly reminding people that the cat's, well, getting on, and could die soon, and saying our grand old cat's dying. Still, I'm glad we had been fairly realistic about it, that latterly we'd never tried to pretend it wasn't just inevitable, but in all probability fairly close at hand. So, when the shock did come, we were all, up to a point at least, forearmed to cope with it.

My wife and my daughter had been out together, shopping I think. When they got back, my son (who, being still pretty small, hadn't fully grasped the situation) and I had to tell them that something had happened to our poor old Whiskers, and that his end was near. He was still coming out with that ghastly and dreadful cry from time to time. My daughter ran into the bathroom and sat down on the floor and broke into floods of tears. 'It isn't fair. It isn't fair,' she kept saying. What could I do? What could I say? I sat there on the edge of the bath. It was so difficult because she had grown up with that cat, and I remembered that one day she had even taken him to her infant school where, naturally, he had been an enormous success. A beautiful and essential part of her formation, of her growth, was now leaving her, and I cried for her and I cried for Whiskers.

I went in to Whiskers. I knelt down by the bed. When he saw me he crawled out from under the bed, dragging himself by his forelegs. I stroked him. I murmured things to him, nonsense probably. He purred. I looked into his eyes. They were different, so soft, so gentle and with a dreamy quality to them. They were so – well, beautiful, and definitely not the eyes of a frightened animal. I don't know what he was seeing, but he wasn't scared.

'Thanks, Whiskers,' I said to him. 'Thanks, Whiskers, for everything.' I can't say why, but I know I'll always be so grateful, for the rest of my life, that I was able to say thanks to my old chum. For everything he had given us.

He died. He died that very same evening, around eight o'clock, and his going was like the rest of his life, elegant, generous, clean. He didn't cause us any suffering. He didn't make us stand around and watch him suffer. He went, just like that. No fuss, no trauma.

I think he lived a long and happy life secure in the company of those who loved him. He sowed his wild oats and he enjoyed an adulthood full of action and variety and the sort of things cats go in for, and he had a tranquil old age, rounding off his long life safe and cosy and in perfect health to the very end. The sort of life that one would wish for all beings, humans included. And then, when his end came, it came suddenly and serenely and, I like to think, painlessly, at the natural termination of his years. And a part of him will continue to live on for a while, because, as long as we live, none of us shall completely forget him.

He is sleeping in a lovely valley in the hills under a pear tree, and Tibby, the cat he saved so many years ago and one of his early loves, is near him, as are several other of his old friends and his offspring. We still drive out to say hi to them all from time to time, and an extra-special hi for him, because we've had many cats since his time, and loved them, but Whiskers was – well, special, and is especially missed.

I've spoken of the life of Whiskers the Cat, and I've also spoken, a little, of his death. Now, before we take our final leave of him, it's time to talk about his miracles. It could seem a bit fatuous to talk about the miracles worked by a humble cat, and it probably is. But the peculiar thing about miracles is that they often depend on how we see them. What might be a miracle for one person may be a mere commonplace event for everyone else. What is perfectly normal for me could well be a miracle of enormous significance for you. It all depends on perspective. And as for those who say that miracles are to be associated only with human beings: well, I have the feeling that certain individuals endowed with a particular affinity with the spirit of nature, or sympathy for animals – such as St Francis of Assisi, or Confucius or Lao Tze, or the Prophet Mohammed – would not be in complete agreement with them.

Miracles are for those who see them as such. And from this perspective I have no scruples in affirming that our old cat, in his own small way, worked miracles.

He brought love into our home. He taught to our children, and to us, benevolence. When, for personal reasons, times were very hard for us, with relationship problems between me and my wife, financial problems, work problems, health problems, stress problems, he was always there. He was always there to set us off laughing, to make us change the subject, to get us talking, to distract us, even if just temporarily, from our preoccupations. In the ridiculous things he did, or in his own problems and difficulties, there was always that small something that helped us to re-dimension, just a little, the problems of our existence. His mere presence was a simple and unequivocal guarantee of warmth and affection. In the midst of our troubles, maybe when my wife and I

were going through a phase of hating each other –
something that, I'm pretty sure, happens from time to
time in most couples – Whiskers was around, keeping
alive that little flame of warmth and goodwill which
would be gradually reinforced and reutilised to
restore harmony between us. Having an animal
around often means that the light of affection is still
burning, however weakly, and will return to shine
more brilliantly and warmly when the difficult times
have passed. To put it another way, a nice and affectionate animal around the house is good for your
health, because he makes you laugh and he makes
you love him. And laughter and love are probably
among the most important things we can have. Think
what life would be like without them: a pretty
gloomy business, when all is said and done. When
I talk about miracles, I'm talking precisely about this
– how it is possible for us to transform the presence
of an animal into something dynamic and life-
renewing, into something that gives us great and
necessary help in many of the difficult moments of
life. And in this, Whiskers beat all the rest of them –
he was The Best.

The other day my wife and I were moving a wardrobe
in our bedroom. We wanted to see what it would be

like against another wall. It's an enormous wardrobe, and we hadn't moved it since we'd first got it, donkey's years ago. Under the wardrobe, in the corner, there were: two marbles, a box of matches, a rubber ball, two little cars from chocolate eggs, two beer-bottle tops, a little bottle of nail-varnish, a pen, a chalk frog, a wooden rabbit, a piece of broken glass, a wooden cube and a rubber.

I felt the tears stinging my eyes. Whiskers's last hidden treasure. We put the wardrobe back in its old place, leaving our old cat's collection undisturbed.

20
Goodnight my sweet cat

Goodnight my sweet cat
Your long summer is over
And the days we enjoyed with you have come to an
    end
Goodnight my sweet cat
And goodnight to the joy you brought us
Goodnight to the warmth of your eyes
And the placid consolation of your presence.

Goodnight my sweet cat
Our journey together is over and now both of us must
    go forward alone
You to the infinite wonder of the sky and the stars

Me, for yet a while longer,
Back to the things you knew and loved so well

Goodbye my sweet cat and goodbye to the summer
You have a long journey to make and I have another
You, back out towards the essence of things
And a blending with the best things of the universe,
I, back home, without you

Goodnight, my sweet cat, goodnight for ever
But I know I'll meet you from time to time
Finding you in the sunniest, warmest rooms of my
   dreams
Eternally purring.

21
The cat's year: autumn

Autumn is the season of the waning of the year, the season in which the nights get longer and cooler and the cats are, morally and physically, preparing themselves for the coming of the winter. So long as they are still vigorous and healthy, the autumn is a most joyful season for them, especially if they live in an area where there are a lot of trees and green around them, because, for many cats, the joy of chasing after falling leaves or rolling about on laboriously raked-together heaps of them is something that will never fade. And a cat dedicated to rolling around in a pile of leaves really is something to watch: it is almost impossible to imagine anything closer to sheer pleasure and fun. There is, indeed, only one thing of this nature that it is even better to see, and that is when there are two or even three cats all busy in the same heap, chasing each other in and out of the leaves, leaping up and down like mad things, out of their minds with excitement and miaowing at the top of their voices.

The weather, too, is more varied and unpredictable than during the rest of the year, so cats often enjoy the opportunity of alternating calm and sunny days with blustery and windy ones, with rainy ones and, if they are lucky, with mists and light fogs to creep through in a sinister manner – and woe betide any small creature that happens to be out wandering around in the mist to enjoy the evening air or heading wearily home with its shopping.

Cats eat lots more, too, in the autumn, though, as far as some of the cats I know are concerned, it is practically impossible to imagine them actually eating more than they do during the rest of the year since they seem to be always at it anyway. But you do see most of them – and here, as in so many other things in the feline world, there are also the honourable exceptions who deserve a mention for their moderation – getting plumper by the day as they store up fat in their bodies to be absolutely sure they will be in the ideal form for facing the chill and the cold if and when it arrives. And here it is that our cats, happily and busily tucking into their dinner, and with very little time for anything else, will take their leave of the reader, thanking you for your polite and discreet company throughout the pages of this book and wishing all the best to you and your family and, naturally, to your pets – especially those of a particular species that it is unnecessary, by now, to name. Observing them munching away happily there makes me feel a bit peckish myself, and I think it would be a sensible (and indeed wise) idea to take the hint and finish off the book here with a nice warm handshake to the reader, and then get up from this desk and have a nice long liberating stretch before going and making myself some dinner too. Yes, even in the simple, everyday things of life, there is considerable wisdom to be gleaned from the observation of cats.